# MASS MEDIA AND INFORMATION REVOLUTION

# MASS MEDIA AND INFORMATION REVOLUTION

Gopal Bhargava

ISHA BOOKS
DELHI—110 033

**Mass Media and Information Revolution**
*(Mass Media)*



ISBN: 978-81-8205-048-8



Published in 2004 in India by
Isha Books, D-43, Prithviraj Road
Adarsh Nagar, Delhi-110 033

*Lasertypesetting by:* Varsha Graphics, Delhi
*Printed at:* Chawla Offset Press, Delhi

# Contents

# Preface

Media are having a pivotal role in informing the people and influencing their thinking and shaping their attitudes. One of their major purposes is to provide an impartial, disinterested synthesis of information. Today, they are undergoing tremendous changes. They are more fashionable, more powerful and more influential today. They are viewed as a means to increase diversity, democracy and empower the individual. However, beneath the overly optimistic image of global cooperation and sharing lies a side of globalization which is generally ignored by the media. There are many unintended and unpredicted side-effects of the information revolution and the spread of mass media.

Today, it is probably easier to set up a worldwide accessible radio or television channel on the Internet than it is to get employment at a traditional broadcasting company. This means that the control of the media production is diverging and that novel, sometimes less traditional content providers, enter the media industry. Information technology changes people's work and it should be emphazised that the informatics interest is to augment people's proficiency rather than to replace them with information technology.

This book encompasses lot of connotations for various concepts connected to mass media. It consists of major aspects of comparison of mass media with interpersonal communication, growth of communication technology, satellite communication, applications of advanced communication technology in agricultural development, traditional folk media and so on. We hope this unique publication would be a useful reference guide for social scientists, educationists, technicians of mass media, research scholars, media personnel, besides, policy-makers, planners and administers at global level too.

***Editor***

# 1

# Information Revolution

The information revolution facilitates interstate cooperation, overlays interstate relations with nonstate relationships in new ways, and reinforces pre-existing relations of power and dominance among states. IR theory, should explain all three kinds of effects, which roughly correspond with the liberal, revolutionary, and conservative world views.

The information revolution in international relations sees the information revolution as making more efficient the various problem-solving functions of international organizations and regimes. In particular, cheap and plentiful information makes a range of collective goods problems somewhat more tractable.

Collective goods problems are central to international relations in all topic areas, most spectacularly in global environmental politics (notably global warming), and obviously throughout IPE (open trade; cartels; currency stability; foreign aid; etc.), but also throughout international security affairs (security dilemmas; arms control; alliance formation; burden sharing; etc.). Information technologies are making these problems less intractable for several reasons:

(1) Transparency makes free riding and double-crossing easier to detect and punish. "Transparency" reduces cheating or free riding (such as on a treaty, alliance, or cartel), because all states know what the others are doing. As evolving information technologies illuminate the world, international regimes should be strengthened. For example, in today's satellite-image world, governments are less likely to ignore evidence of pending invasions of their countries, as did Soviet leaders in 1941 and Israeli leaders in 1973.

(2) Telecommunications and computers make the administration of complex international organizations and agreements more cost-effective. New, historical forms of organization - above all the European Union and the United Nations, rely on these capabilities. The regimes dealing with information flows themselves have been among the most successful regimes historically. The longest-established IOs are specialized agencies dealing with technical aspects of international coordination such as aviation and postal exchange, such as the International Telecommunications Union (ITU), the Universal Postal Union (UPU), and the World Meteorological Association (WMO).

(3) More accurate information makes rational calculations more reliable (mitigating some well-known psychological barriers to rational actions in a mixed-interest game, including various misperceptions, information screens, and gaps in

intelligence data). Furthermore, as the costs of seeking and processing information decline, "satisficing" outcomes come closer to optimal ones. Similarly, information technologies mitigate the time constraints that prevent full assessment of available information, especially in crises. U.S. Defense Secretary William Cohen said in 1997: "The unrelenting flow of information, the need to digest it on a minute-by-minute basis, is quite different from anything I've experienced before. . . . There's little time for contemplation; most of it is action."During the Cold War, information infrastructure served as a confidence-building measure for the management of potential crises. The hot line connected the U.S. and Soviet leaders in real time. The later agreement on incidents at sea provided for efforts to control escalation after a hostile encounter or accident on the high seas. Eventually, the superpowers developed elaborate centers and systems for the exchange of information in a crisis.

(4) Information technologies are lowering transaction costs and making world markets more efficient and more tightly integrated, creating incentives for international cooperation to realize the economic benefits of trade. For example, thanks to the information revolution, more than a trillion dollars each day crosses borders in international currency markets, which are privately operated. Better information means more efficient markets. In effect, by making global trade more profitable, the information revolution is increasing the joint part of the payoff relative to the individual part, in the mixed-interest game. Interdependence alters the cost-benefit calculations of national leaders so as to make military leverage less attractive.

Information technologies are empowering nonstate actors in new ways, as well as fueling "globalization" with its various ramifications. Newly empowered individuals and groups have begun to create new transnational networks worldwide, bypassing states.Telecommunications and computerization allow economics, politics, and culture alike to operate on a global scale as never before.

One aspect of the challenge is the changing nature of territoriality. The territorial nature of the interstate system reflects the origins of that system in an age when agrarian societies relied on agriculture to generate wealth. In today's world, where trade and technology rather than land create wealth, the territorial state matters less. Information-based economies are linked across borders instantly, and the idea of the state as having a hard shell seems archaic.

Israel's successful defense of its borders could not stop Iraqi scud missiles from hitting Israeli cities during the Gulf War. In international environmental politics, the effects of the information revolution go further. The industrial revolution, which harnessed fossil fuels to power machinery, changed IR profoundly.

Now, perhaps, a comparable revolution in technology may mark the end of industrialization and raise the possibility for the global South to bypass industrialization and the North to decrease its energy use, thus reducing global warming.

Similarly, telecommunications could change the path of development in poor countries, possibly bypassing traditional infrastructure like phone lines and leapfrogging to a wireless networked economy. In Africa, cheap cell phones with cheap prepaid calling cards have let millions of relatively poor individuals bypass the lack of infrastructure previously needed to communicate.

In the green revolution, such practices were often dismissed as superstitious nonsense and replaced with modern water-allocation schemes. But the water priests actually had more experience with local conditions over many years, and more legitimacy with the local farmers, than did the foreign experts. A U.S. anthropologist recently developed graphical software for Macintosh computers that the water priests could use to gain access to technical information about water supplies without sacrificing their own experience and authority.

In this way, information technology provided tools to empower local culture. Cultural effects of the information revolution are also far-reaching. There are about one and a half billion TV sets and two and a half billion radio receivers in the world. The Qatar-based all-news satellite TV network, al Jazeera, begun in 1996, reaches an influential audience across the region and world. The only foreign network allowed to report regularly from Taliban-ruled Afghanistan during the 2001 U.S. bombing, its office there was destroyed by a U.S. missile.

The fact that Israeli- Palestinian conflicts play out regionally and globally in the media make the Palestinian issue a top priority even for citizens of Arab countries not materially affected by the conflict. For example, TV footage of a 12-year-old Palestinian being fatally shot as his father pleaded with Israeli soldiers to stop shooting, was replayed repeatedly on Arab TV and deepened anti-Israeli sentiment as the second Intifada gathered steam in September 2000.

Of course, information crossing borders on mass media is not always accurate. A poignant example came in 1991, when Albania's communist government was crumbling along with its economy. Desperately poor Albanians rode overloaded ferries to nearby Italy. As it turned out, Albanians had an exaggerated view of Italian prosperity. Albanians had been seen Italian TV commercials in which cats were fed their dinners on silver platters.

Information can be used against governments by foreign governments and domestic political opponents alike. When allowed to circulate among a population, ideas become a powerful force that can sweep aside governments, as when the idea of democracy swept away the white-rule system of apartheid in South Africa in the early 1990s. Television coverage fed popular discontent regarding the U.S. war in Vietnam in the 1960s and 1970s, and the Russian war in Chechnya in 1995.

In Iran, the government was brought down in part by audiotapes containing speeches and sermons by Ayatollah Khomeini, who spoke against the inequalities and harsh repression of the pro-Western government of the Shah of Iran. The power of his sermons could not have been captured in newspapers and pamphlets. In Thailand in 1992, military leaders lost power in what some Thais called "the cellular phone revolution."

When the government shot the demonstrators in the streets, arrested them, and cut off their phone lines, the protesters stayed organized by using mobile phones and fax machines. In the Philippines in 2001, huge protests that swept a president from office were organized through text messages on cell phones. The phones are used by 2 million Filipinos including some homelessv people.

The harsh military government in Burma (Myanmar) faced the power of shortwave radio broadcasts by the opposition movement, made using a transmitter owned by the government of Norway. In Ghana, very popular talk-shows on private FM radio programs-allowed after 1995-gave voice to ordinary people who then threw out the ruling party in 2000.

Government efforts to counteract such uses of information seem to be losing a race with evolving technologies. For example, China and several other developing countries have channeled all access to the Internet (and the World Wide Web) through a few state-controlled service providers, but enterprising Chinese citizens can hack their way through these controls.

Already 15 million Chinese are Internet users, and hundreds of millions more may join them within a few years. During and after the 1989 Tiananmen protests, before the Internet was a factor, the Chinese government stationed police at every fax machine in the country to screen incoming faxes after foreigners began faxing in reports of the shooting of protesters in Beijing. Even for a police state, this is a burden on both the police and the fax users, and would be a doomed effort today.

In the bigger picture, it is unclear whether the ongoing Chinese opening of its economy to the world, a process that opens channels of information, can coexist with continued political authoritarianism under communist rule. The Soviet Union during the Cold War prohibited all but a few photocopy machines. Dissidents' writings were passed from hand to hand and recopied on typewriters.

In 1987 the Soviet Union had only 16 international long-distance circuits in and out of the country, all routed through Moscow. This helped the government to reduce the influence of foreign ideas and to closely monitor foreigners-but at a huge cost in economic efficiency. Soviet efforts to control information did not prevent collapse of that society.

Rather, the effort to run a modern economy without photocopy machines, international phone lines, computers, and other information technologies clearly contributed to economic collapse. The forging of transnational communities and supranational identities-a process familiar to students of the EU-is spreading widely.

Riding the telecommunications revolution, a global culture is beginning to develop, notwithstanding the great divisions remaining in culture and perspective (especially between the rich and poor regions of the world. Across dozens of countries, people are tuned in to the same news, the same music, the same sports events.

Along with international politics, these activities now take place on a world stage with a world audience. The process might be seen as a form of cultural integration, similar to economic and technical integration. Ultimately, transnational cultural integration might lead to the emergence of supranational identities, including a global identity.

Nationalism has tapped into the psychological dynamics of group identity in a powerful way that has legitimized the state as the ultimate embodiment of its people's aspirations and identity. Now the information revolution may aid the development of supranational identity. Global identity has not yet come to rival national identity in any state. For a fleeting moment at the turn of the millennium such a global identity seemed almost possible.

The feared "Y2K" computer bug, which would cause old software to think time had jumped back 100 years, was fixed in a massive technology upgrade that "leveraged the resources of the whole planet," in the words of an IBM executive. On December 31, 1999, as each time zone passed midnight, people around the world watched to see whether fears of computer failures, terrorist attacks, or riots would materialize.

UN Secretary-General Annan said that "each city seemed to be rooting for cities in the next time zone to get through Y2K without any problems. It was like, 'O.K., Tokyo is through, now how about Beijing?' And then, 'Moscow is through, how about New York?' For one brief moment there was a pulling together all over the planet."As the feared problems did not materialize, the world was left with a 24-hour moment of good feeling broadcast live on CNN and the Internet.

Although a global culture is still only nascent and the most powerful identity is still at the national level, people have begun to participate in specific communities that bridge national boundaries. International journalists, for example, are members of such a community. Though a journalist's identity as a journalist rarely takes precedence over his or her national identity, the existence of the transnational community of journalists creates a new form of international interdependence.

Like journalists, scientists and church members work in communities spanning national borders. So do members of transnational movements, such as those linking women from various countries, or environmentalists, or human rights activists. The effect once again is to undermine the state's role as the primary actor in international affairs.

More important, the links forged in such transnational epistemic communities may create a new functionalism that could encourage international integration on a global scale. International sports competition is one of the broadest-based transnational communities, especially strong at the regional level. Of course, international sports competition can stir up animosities between neighbors, as when British soccer hooligans rampage through other European countries after their team loses a game.

But sports also create a sense of participation in a supranational community. This is especially true of world-level sports events in which a global athletic community participates. The Olympic Games are a global event broadcast to a worldwide audience. The U.S.-Chinese rapprochement of 1971 was so delicate that political cooperation was impossible until the way had first been paved by sports-the U.S. table tennis team that made the first official U.S. visit to China.

The U.S. wrestling team's visit to Iran several years ago also opened new doors. Music is also becoming globalized. People who cannot understand each other's languages can understand each other's music. And tourism also builds transnational communities. International tourists cross borders 500 million times a year. Tourism ranks among the top export industries worldwide. Added to these contacts are exchange students and those who attend college in a foreign country.

The Internet now allows transnational dialogues to take place at a global level. The World Wide Web allows people to move seamlessly around the world. Significantly, the Web creates organizing structures and communities that can be almost totally divorced from physical location, bringing together people with common cultural or economic interest from anywhere in the world.

The Internet in many ways empowers small fringe groups relative to states, and leaves states vulnerable in new ways. Hackers have taken over control of U.S. government computers and have unleashed costly viruses against businesses and people worldwide. These cyberattacks by small-scale actors may target foreign countries. Thousands of Israeli teenagers attacked Web sites in the Arab world, and Arab hackers knocked out Israeli sites in return, during the violent "Intifada II" of Fall 2000.

During the U.S.-China "spy plane" standoff in 2001, nationalistic Chinese hackers claimed to have put pro-Chinese graffiti on 1,000 U.S. Web sites, and U.S. hackers returned the favor. An Ohio school district found that its site now played China's national anthem. The Chinese communist party criticized "Web terrorism" and the crisis eased. After September 11, however, the U.S. government worried that real terrorists could use the Internet to cause massive disruptions in U.S. economic life.

The transnational connections forged by various communities-sports, music, tourism, and so forth-deepen the international interdependence that links the well-being of one state to that of other states. This may promote peace, because a person who knows more about a foreign country and has developed empathy for its culture is likely to reject political conflict with that country and support positive cooperation with it.

But sometimes cultural contact increases awareness of differences, creating distrust. Thus, as the information revolution unfolds, it increases international interdependence, making actions in one state reverberate in other states more strongly than in the past. Information is thus slowly undermining the assumptions of state sovereignty and territorial integrity held dear by realists. At the same time, by empowering substate and transnational actors, information technology is undermining the centrality of states themselves in world affairs.

Although the liberal and revolutionary effects of the information revolution receive most attention, a more conservative set of effects also deserve study. Information capabilities are new and powerful tools in the hands of the richest and most powerful actors, especially states and above all the world's superpower. During the past decade of intense development of information technology, the United States has dominated the uses of these potentials-economically, culturally, and militarily.

That the unprecedented information revolution coincides with the unprecedented increase in hegemonic power by the world's most powerful state. First, information-based changes in military forces are empowering both the world's superpower and small groups like terrorists, but on balance the strong are getting stronger. Military historians refer to a period of rapid change in the conduct of war as a "revolution in military affairs." These periods usually combine innovative applications of new technology with changes in military doctrine, organization, or operations.

Such revolutions may arise from innovations in organization, as when revolutionary France first mobilized an entire nation into a war machine two centuries ago. Or they may arise from new military doctrine, as when Germany used the "blitzkrieg" to overwhelm Poland and France at the outset of World War II, or from technology alone, as with the invention of nuclear weapons. Many military analysts consider the present period, starting with the 1991 Gulf War, to be a revolution in military affairs, especially in U.S. forces.

Management of information is central to this revolution. Clausewitz's famous "fog of war" refers to the confusion and uncertainty that greatly reduces the effectiveness of armies in battle. Today's U.S. forces are piercing that fog for themselves while thickening it for their enemies. As the fog of war becomes transparent, U.S. forces can also disperse light forces widely, rather than massing concentrations of heavy units as Clausewitz emphasized.

The ability to conduct precision strikes and the increasing use of space in warfare are two other aspects of the present revolution. The revolutionary potentials were first apparent in the lopsided 1991 victory over Iraq's army, which was very large and well-equipped but not technologically advanced.

The 1999 Kosovo campaign was notable in achieving its war aims without loss of a single U.S. life to hostile fire. But the revolution was best exemplified in the 2001 Afghanistan campaign. Small groups of lightly armed U.S. special forces, inserted across the country, used lasers to illuminate targets for smart bombs dropped by high-flying aircraft that never touched Afghan soil.

The integration of these diverse forces using information-rich battle management systems resulted in a stunningly effective bombing campaign that destroyed the Taliban as an effective army and handed victory to the smaller anti-Taliban armies, all with just a handful of U.S. casualties. Critics worry that the revolution has brought an unrealistic expectation of low U.S. casualties, which may make political leaders unduly cautious in applying military force.

For example, at the end of the Afghanistan campaign, terrorist leaders including Osama bin Laden slipped away as the United States relied on local warlords to hunt them, when larger numbers of U.S. troops might have captured them (with U.S. casualties). A more unsettling thought is that the revolution in military affairs may work for the terrorists as well.

The September 11 attackers used information technology, such as encrypted Internet communications, to coordinate forces while keeping U.S. authorities in the dark. They carried out precision strikes over long distances with very small, dispersed units. As a result, 19.attackers killed more than 3,000 people, and an expenditure of under $1 million caused tens of billions of dollars in damage.

Admittedly, a counter-current in the information revolution works against U.S. military predominance. Electronics are changing the costs and relative capabilities of weapons across the board. Computer chips in guided missiles have made them a formidable weapon on land, sea, and air. The miniaturization of such weaponry is making smaller and cheaper military forces more powerful than ever.

An infantry soldier now can use a shoulder-fired missile costing $10,000 to destroy a main battle tank costing $1 million. Similarly, a small boat firing an antiship missile costing $250,000 can potentially destroy a major warship costing hundreds of millions of dollars. The U.S.-made Stinger antiaircraft missile-portable and shoulder-launched-helped turn the tide against the Soviet Union in the war in Afghanistan in the 1980s, with far-reaching consequences.

Land-based Chinese missiles could destroy expensive U.S. aircraft carriers in a conflict over Taiwan. New Chinese anti-aircraft systems reportedly can detect even "stealth" U.S. aircraft while remaining passive and thus not presenting a target. To take advantage of new information technologies, U.S. forces are developing new battlefield tactics calling for smaller, more mobile weapons and troop units, along with more unmanned systems, linked by intensive communications networks.

Unmanned drones in Afghanistan in 2001 monitored Taliban movements from the air, and were retrofitted with two remote-controlled missiles. Within the decade, the U.S. military may begin deploying a new generation of laser weapons fired from planes at targets on the ground. Strategies for cyberwar-disrupting enemy computer networks to degrade command-and-control, or even hacking into bank accounts electronically-were developed by NATO forces during the 1999 Kosovo war, though mostly not implemented, and will probably figure in future wars.

Information is crucial to the military uses of outer space, where again the United States holds an overwhelming advantage. Space forces are military forces designed to attack in or from outer space. Only the

United States and Russia have substantial military capabilities in space. China plans to join the manned-space club by 2005, though with far fewer capabilities overall.

The development of space weapons has been constrained by the technical challenges and expenses of space operations, and by norms against militarizing space. U.S. policy makers in 2001 announced a plan to begin testing space-based lasers (for intercepting ballistic missiles) in several years. Satellites perform military surveillance and mapping, communications, weather assessment, and early warning of ballistic missile launches.

Satellites also provide navigational information to military forces-army units, ships, planes, and even guided missiles in flight. Poorer states can buy satellite photos on the commercial market-including high-resolution pictures that Russia sells for hard currency. Similarly, handheld receivers for the U.S. Global Positioning System (GPS), a network of 18 satellites, are available commercially, so the military forces of any country can ride free on the GPS.

But in general outer space is an area in which great powers have great advantages over smaller or poorer states. The information revolution is also enhancing various means of intelligence gathering. For example, in 1999 a Russian spy taped conversations from a listening device planted in a high-level conference room at the U.S. State Department. Again, the United States holds the advantage since it operates massive intelligence-gathering operations.

Satellite intelligence is supplemented by monitoring of a very high volume of electronic communications, such as radio and telephone conversations. Terrorists in remote Afghanistan had to use couriers because the U.S. military could monitor their electronic communications. In 2001, a U.S. reconnaissance airplane eavesdropping along the Chinese coast made an emergency landing in Chinese territory after being bumped by a Chinese fighter jet.

China held the crew for weeks to protest U.S. surveillance. (And China enjoyed an intelligence bonanza by examining the U.S. plane.) Chinese protests in part reflected the insecurity of China (and other countries) in the face of the American ability to suck up huge amounts of intelligence without ever crossing the Chinese border. Altogether, the budgets of U.S. intelligence agencies were around $27 billion in 1998.

The National Security Agency (NSA), responsible for encoding and codebreaking, is believed to have the most powerful computer facility in the world. Clearly, intelligence operations taken together are very large and are growing in importance as the information revolution proceeds and as the war on terrorism makes their mission more central.

Beyond military affairs, another conservative aspect of the information revolution is the "digital divide," especially between the global North and South. The rich get richer, and the information revolution is no exception. Richer countries have much greater access to information technologies than do poorer ones. The information revolution may give the industrialized West more power than ever, and increase the North-South gap in wealth.

Just as industrial infrastructure is located mostly in the North, so is the world's information infrastructure. While a generation of students in industrialized countries go online, poorer countries still struggle to extend literacy to rural populations. Nearly half the adults in South Asia, Africa, and the Middle East are illiterate, compared with fewer than 10 percent in some middle-income third world countries, and fewer than 5 percent in the industrialized West.

Furthermore, as the Internet wires parts of the world into a tight network centered on the United States, other regions are largely left out. Poor countries and poor people cannot afford computers-the equivalent of eight years' wages for a typical Bangladeshi, for example. Users of the World Wide Web in 2001 made up 26 percent of the population in the United States, 7 percent in Russia, and 1 percent in South Asia, the Middle East, and Africa. The worldwide community of Web users was 40 percent North American with Europeans and Asia-Pacific splitting most of the remainder.

English is the language of a strong majority of Web sites worldwide, even though non-English speakers now make up a slight majority of Web users. Even the architecture of cyberspace assumes the United States as the default in such domain names as .gov (U.S. government) and .mil (U.S. military). Just from 1999 to 2001, Internet users increased from 150 million to.400 million worldwide. This explosive growth is mainly occurring among the richest strata of the world's people, however.

Some activists hope that the Internet can transform poor villages in the global South, partly by letting them produce traditional goods locally and market them globally. The UN ECOSOC hopes to place an Internet computer within a mile of most of the world's villages, to be funded by $1 billion in hoped-for contributions (that seem unlikely to materialize in full).

A model project in Cambodia in 2001 helped revive a village silk-weaving industry by marketing locally made scarves on a village Web site. However, look more closely at this "model": The project was feasible only because a satellite company owned by the Thai prime minister donated $18,000 per year of link time. A U.S. aid organization provided the computers, training, Web site design, and credit-card processing required to sell scarves from the village.

The reality is that most poor villages cannot afford the Internet, cannot read the language of most Web sites, and cannot maintain computers and Web sites without extensive training. A similar effect marks the rise of global culture, which is primarily the culture of white Europeans and their descendants in rich areas of the world. For many people, especially in the global South, the information revolution carrying global culture into their midst is, despite its empowering potential, an invasive force in practice-cultural imperialism.

Because cultures are being subsumed, half of the world's nearly 7,000 languages risk extinction this century, according to UNESCO. Above all, the emerging global culture is dominated by the world's superpower, the United States, whose cultural influence is at least as strong as U.S. military influence. If there is a world language, it is English. U.S. films and TV shows dominate world markets. For instance, U.S. movies predominate in countries from Europe to Asia to Latin America.

Governments spend large amounts of money and effort trying to gain information about what is happening both inside and outside their territories. They keep files on their citizens ranging from social security records to secret police files. They compile economic statistics to chart their own economic health and make estimates of the economic health of other states. Most operate intelligence-gathering agencies.

With today's information technologies, it is easier for governments to gather, organize, and store huge amounts of information. In this respect, the information revolution empowers governments more than ever. In the past, a wanted criminal, druglord, or terrorist could slip over the border and take refuge in a foreign country. The terrorists who attacked the United States in 2001 demonstrated how easy this was.

Today, however, it is more likely that a routine traffic ticket in the foreign country could trigger an instant directive to arrest the person. Information technologies give repressive governments more power to keep tabs on citizens, spy on dissidents, and manipulate public opinion. Those technologies are now also being mobilized in force to strengthen international counterterrorism.

Of course, as the cost of information technology decreases, it comes into reach of more states. The great powers have always been able to maintain a worldwide presence and gather information globally. Now small states can gain some of the same capabilities electronically-if only by monitoring world affairs on CNN. Governments also seek to control information.

Most governments own and operate at least one main TV station, and many hold a monopoly on TV stations. Thus TV signals often rank with military equipment and currency as capabilities so important to a government that it must control them itself. Indeed, in a military coup d'état, usually one of the first and most important targets seized is the television broadcasting facility. When power is up for grabs in a state, it is now as likely that fighting will occur in the government TV studios or at the transmitting antenna as at the legislature or presidential offices.

As the Soviet Union broke up in the early 1990s, TV towers were the scene of confrontations in several republics. In Lithuania, a crowd of Lithuanian nationalists surrounded the TV tower, and Soviet troops killed a dozen people shooting their way in. During the 2001 U.S.-Chinese crisis regarding the U.S. reconnaissance plane, the Chinese government heavily jammed broadcasts into China of VOA and Radio Free Asia. U.S. military leaders recognized the importance of playing to a global audience when, during the bombing of Bosnian Serb forces in 1995, they designated an ammunition dump close to Sarajevo the "CNN site" because they knew the explosion would make good footage for Sarajevo-based TV cameras.

During the Gulf War, the U.S. military fed TV networks pictures of precision weapons striking their targets, to help "sanitize" the bombing campaign (which mostly used unguided bombs). Governments spread false as well as true information as a means of international influence. This is called disinformation.

In the 1930s, the Nazis discovered that the "big lie," if repeated enough times, would be accepted as truth by most people. It is harder to fool international audiences.these days, but domestic ones can still respond to propagandistic misinformation. Because of the need for public support, even authoritarian governments spend great effort on propaganda-the public promotion of their official line-to win support for foreign policies.

States use television, newspapers, and other information media in this effort. For instance, when China invited President Nixon to visit in 1972, the Chinese government mounted a major propaganda campaign to explain to its people that the United States was not so bad after all. In many countries the state owns or controls major mass media such as television and newspapers, mediating the flow of information to its citizens; however, new information technologies with multiple channels make this harder to do.

In democracies, where governments must stand for election, public opinion is even more important. An unpopular war can force a leader or party from office, as happened to U.S. President Johnson in 1968 during the Vietnam War. Or a popular war can help secure a government's mandate to continue in power, as happened to Margaret Thatcher in Britain after the 1982 Falkland Islands War.

A key influence on public opinion is the content of scenes appearing on television: U.S. soldiers were sent to Somalia to assist in relief efforts in 1992 after TV news showed the heartrending results of civil war and famine there. But after TV news showed an American soldier's body being dragged through the streets by members of a Somali faction after a deadly firefight that killed 18 U.S. soldiers, public opinion shifted quickly against the Somalia operation.

During the war in Bosnia, officials in the U.S. State Department said privately that the main goal of U.S. policy was often just to keep the conflict there off of the front pages of U.S. newspapers (an elusive goal, as it turned out). Journalists serve as the gatekeepers of information passing from foreign policy elites to the public.

The media and government often conflict, because of the traditional role of the press as a watchdog and critic of government actions and powers. The media try to uncover and publicize that which the government wants to hide, especially in situations such as the Iran-Contra scandal. Foreign policy decision makers also rely on the media for information about foreign affairs.

Yet the media also depend on government for information; the size and resources of the foreign policy bureaucracies dwarf those of the press. These advantages give the government great power to manipulate journalists by feeding them information, in order to shape the news and influence public opinion. Government decision makers can create dramatic stories in foreign relations-through summit meetings, crises, actions, and so forth. Bureaucrats can also leak secret information to the press in order to support their own point of view and win bureaucratic battles.

Finally, the military and the press have a running battle about journalists' access to military operations; for instance, in the invasion of Grenada and the Gulf War, U.S. military censors limited media coverage. One outcome of the Cold War was the victory of "free" countries over those whose governments tried to know about and control all aspects of their citizens' lives.

In communist societies like East Germany, the ruthless secret police kept files on everyone, had informers on every block,.and monitored the streets with video cameras. With right-wing totalitarianism having been defeated in World War II earlier, it seemed that free societies were the rule. See-all-and-know-all government was a thing of the past. Yet, the information revolution delivered into the hands of governments tremendous new power to extend the reach of government surveillance both horizontally (to every square foot of distant countries) and vertically (peering into what had been private places in citizens' lives).

The United States, which had the most advanced technology, also had the most finely developed checks and balances on government power to prevent the abuse of information technology and preserve citizens' right to privacy. The changes in world order since September 11 have changed this balance between the state's responsibility to provide security and individuals' rights to not have the government constantly looking over their shoulders.

Today's world order is one of profound vulnerability-in which a few people in a remote country can change the tenor of life in the world's superpower. In response to the threat of terrorism, U.S. law-enforcement agencies began to expand and network together surveillance systems, such as video cameras in public locations. Washington, DC, installed a control room to monitor video feeds from around the city and track suspicious persons or objects.

Tampa, Florida, operated face-recognition software to identify matches between a database of suspects and faces caught on security cameras in a popular shopping district. Privacy advocates argue that these governmental intrusions into traditionally private areas of life undermine the values that America was founded on.

We live in an age when authorities can listen to phone calls and e-mails in volume, peer behind walls with infrared detectors, examine bodily fluids by using drug tests, and scan carry-on luggage with x-rays. Since September 11, governments have used these powers more freely, and citizens have largely acquiesced.

## Information Verification

Developments in information and communication technology (ICT) are driving transformations in the economic, political and military spheres. Powered by the forces of global capital, this trend is unstoppable, although its direction can to some extent be guided. The challenge for the verification community is to exploit the benefits of the information revolution, rather than allow it to create a whole new set of problems.

Advances in information technology (IT) and its convergence with sophisticated communications systems are ushering in what has been labelled an 'information age' or 'knowledge age'. It is argued that contemporary societies, led by the West, are being reshaped into 'knowledge societies'. The concept of the information age demonstrates the evolution from industrial-age manufacturing, through service-based production, to an information economy.

The idea of a knowledge society reflects the perception that information is no longer just a resource, like capital, labour and land, but that it is increasingly the resource. There is widespread scepticism about the extent, pace and consequences of this information revolution. Some observers argue that the Internet economy has failed to have a deep impact, even in the US. Others contend that the level of technological change that was achieved in the first half of the twentieth century had more far reaching social, political and economic ramifications than the digital revolution of recent decades.

The digital revolution of the 1980s and 1990s, along with associated commercial and political developments, has had a major impact on one aspect of international security that is of particular relevance to verification: intelligence. Intelligence can be defined as 'refined, analysed and assessed information'. It is important to stress that intelligence is about providing actionable data to decision-makers to help them understand a certain situation. Although covert sources and methods are often emphasised, these should not be at the core of the activity—they are tools that may add value to more openly collected documentation. Intelligence is at the heart of verification.

Confidence- and security-building measures (CSBMs) are about enhancing transparency between potential adversaries, and arms control regimes are reliant on mutually acceptable and reliable compliance mechanisms, which are underpinned by trusted data. In the past, certain organisations, such as the International Atomic Energy Agency (IAEA) and the United Nations (UN), have shied away from the concept. But, today, they are increasingly coming to accept that intelligence is central to their success and credibility.

The information revolution, which is defined to include associated commercial and political changes, has an impact on intelligence in two broad areas.

First, the digitisation of data, along with increases in processing power, communication bandwidth, and the production of sophisticated software, has made it possible to filter, collate, store, retrieve, manipulate and disseminate information more effectively and faster than ever before.

Second, the combination of new technologies, the commercialisation of previously classified technology and political change has led to an exponential increase in the amount of data available from 'open sources'. Institutions like the media and academia have always been used by defence and foreign affairs intelligence agencies. However, the division between 'white' (open) and 'black' (closed, proprietary or classified) information was previously seen by the Western intelligence community as approximately an 80:20 split. This ratio may now be 90:6:4 between 'white', 'black', and 'grey' information.

The implications of these developments for verification can usefully be discussed in the context of the traditional intelligence process, as used by most defence and national intelligence organisations. This process is based on a model for the development of intelligence or actionable knowledge, which starts with the structured identification of a consumer's needs, recognition of information gaps and the formulation of a collection plan. The documentation is then analysed before it is distributed to the consumer, providing the opportunity for further refinement of the information requirements.

## The Process of Information Verification

The process is often constructed as a cycle, involving the following steps:

- planning and direction;
- collection;
- processing;
- production and analysis;
- assessment; and
- dissemination.

For now, it is helpful to focus on the effect that the information revolution has had on the second, third, fourth and sixth phases of the cycle. Planning and direction have been less affected by the information revolution so they will not be discussed here. And assessment remains at root a cognitive activity that is least affected by technological change.

## Collection

The most obvious impact of the information revolution is on the collection of data for verification of arms control and disarmament regimes and export controls, as well as for use as CSBMs.

Open sources— available commercially or sometimes at no cost— now provide much of the information that is needed to monitor both the intentions and capabilities of states and sub-state groups that are either party to a regime or are of concern to the international community. A proliferation of news sources and electronic discussion channels gives access to large amounts of data on the politics, policies and deliberations of all but the most closed regimes and tightly centralised sub-state bodies.

The interpretation of information on the intentions and world views of governments and other organisations remains as difficult an analytical task as ever, although the open source revolution has at least provided the mass of documentation for analysts to work on. It is important, of course, not to focus exclusively on the 'new' sources and channels enabled by ICT.

A lot of this data will be available from 'traditional' sources, such as scholars, journalists, activists and business travellers. However, the communications revolution, the political opening up of much of the world and economic globalisation have combined to increase the amount and quality of information that 'traditional' human sources can provide.

Meanwhile, very high-resolution commercial satellite imagery (CSI) can be used to monitor physical observables, like troop deployments, border violations and the construction of industrial facilities needed for production of weapons of mass destruction (WMD).

The availability of CSI also results from technological change (the miniaturisation of satellites and sensors, improvements and cost reductions in interpretation software, and better dissemination channels) and geopolitical and economic developments . The outcome is that anybody with the necessary financial and organisational resources can obtain imagery intelligence which approaches the quality enjoyed by the superpowers in the 1970s.

Information from commercial databases and specialist news services can be used to assess shipping movements and trade flows in regard to export controls or sanctions monitoring. Similar sources can be used to examine the activities of potential front companies and efforts to violate sanction regimes.

At the same time, tracking the movements of individuals is becoming much easier. An increasing number of everyday tasks leave 'digital footprints' that are being exploited by commercial marketers and intelligence organisations.

Efforts to 'modernise' government— which most advanced countries are engaged in—will have the effect (notwithstanding data protection legislation) of giving intelligence organisations far more comprehensive pictures of the activities of citizens without recourse to clandestine methods, such as physical or electronic surveillance. This has dramatic ramifications for the monitoring of people and of small groups that are of concern, for instance, in relation to arms proliferation.

### *Processing, production and analysis*

Analysis is at the root of the intelligence process. It is the activity most vulnerable to human error and least subject to technological 'fixes'. The majority of intelligence 'failures' are due to the foundering either of analysis or of understanding by decision-makers, rather than to a breakdown in collection.

For any organisation engaged in processing and analysing data for verification, it is ultimately the quality and mindset of its analysts, combined with the analyst–consumer interface, that determine success or failure. Nonetheless, the information revolution is having a significant impact on this part of the intelligence process.

This capability is advancing rapidly in the commercial world. Retail businesses, including supermarkets, have invested heavily in 'data warehouses' that store giga-bytes of customer information. This is analysed by data mining technologies, which identify, for instance, fraudulent credit card use or food purchasing trends.

Similar technologies are being developed and applied by law enforcement agencies to profile criminal behaviour. And part of the 'joined-up' system of government in countries like the UK is the effort to combine data sets on citizens— held by government agencies— so that individual behaviour can be tracked and monitored. The objective is to provide better services for people and to prevent criminal actions.

Developments in processing and analytical technologies are at least as important for verification as changes in open sources. Intelligent technologies allow the mass of data provided by the open source revolution to be exploited effectively.

Without automated instruments, human analysts would be unable to filter, collate, store, mine and analyse this deluge of information. Furthermore, the production of advanced software tools makes analytical capabilities much more widely available.

Whereas in the recent past it was only specialist public sector organisations, such as the US National Security Agency, the UK Government Communications Headquarters and the Australian Defence Signals Directorate that had access to these technologies, they are now routinely employed by small- and medium-sized enterprises and local law enforcement agencies. Given the rate and pace of change in IT, the effectiveness and ease of use of such tools are likely to increase rapidly.

### *Dissemination*

Presentation and dissemination are an often overlooked part of the intelligence process. However, Western agencies have had to pay more attention to these issues. Intelligence staff at the North Atlantic Treaty Organization (NATO), for instance, often complain that their political decision-makers act on Cable News Network (CNN)'s unanalysed and hastily distributed data, rather than waiting for more considered assessments from the formal intelligence process.

To facilitate the speedy dissemination of well-presented intelligence products, the US intelligence community has responded by taking the lead in exploiting new technologies, such as the Internet Protocol, Hyper Text Mark-up Language (HTML) and video conferencing. The aim is to get analysed work to consumers faster, and to enable consumers to interact with analysts and to arrive jointly at conclusions systematically, supported by an audited reasoning process.

In addition, new technologies are being used to display data in a range of formats, text and images, that facilitate understanding and new ways of considering problems. While these technologies and approaches should make established state intelligence organisations more effective, the point is that they involve commercial off-the-shelf systems. Indeed, many of the tools and techniques now being employed have their origins in the entertainment industry or the financial sector, and, as a result, are available to everyone.

Some non-governmental groups, including political and environmental activists, have, in fact, made more effective use of communication and dissemination technologies than have government organisations. This has a significant effect on verification by empowering a range of actors, such as the media, activists, and intergovernmental bodies and non-governmental organisations (NGOs), and by allowing them to construct robust and responsive regional and global information networks.

### *Strategic implications*

The information revolution is having major ramifications on the sourcing, processing and dissemination of intelligence for those bodies undertaking monitoring and verification. For major governments with established intelligence bureaucracies, one can conclude that these trends will make verification easier.

However, the information revolution has some more interesting strategic implications that will affect verification. The most significant of these are the effects on the information power differential and on the role of third parties.

Information power has been broadly described as the sum of a country's resources that it can use to mould the global information environment, just as military power shapes the physical space. Some strategists argue that the information age plays to the strengths of the US and that the country will have a global advantage in terms of 'hard' military and 'soft' information power. Similarly, in specific regions, states that have the appropriate social, educational, political, and technological foundations are likely to be better placed to exploit the information revolution, and thereby strengthen their information dominance over rivals.

The rise of open sources and the diffusion through globalised commercial channels of ICT for gathering, analysing, and disseminating intelligence have put powerful intelligence capabilities into the hands of even NGOs and technologically backward and impoverished countries. This will go a long way towards countering the information imbalances between parties to CSBMs or arms control treaties, and make it much easier for all sides to an agreement to gather, analyse and share data equitably.

There could be three specific outcomes to this trend.

First, all parties to an accord can have access to the intelligence capabilities that were previously monopolised by the superpowers or regional hegemons. This is likely to have an impact on the willingness of states to enter into agreements and the structure of the verification regime that is put in place.

Second, the increased role of open sources of information and commercially available processing tools should make it easier for countries to share data. National intelligence agencies that are reliant on their own sources and methods will always be reluctant to share documentation and intelligence. But CSBMs and arms control regimes rely on transparency and information sharing; squaring this circle has been a vital but tricky part of past CSBMs and arms control processes. The information revolution eases this problem. For instance, an increasingly popular concept is that of regional conflict prevention, involving crisis monitoring centres.

In the mid-1990s, the Association of South-East Asian Nations (ASEAN) Regional Forum mooted the concept and it also emerged during the Middle East arms control and regional security talks. But this concept has been hindered by credibility problems. Quite simply, states that do not yet trust one another are loath to allow such a facility to have access to sensitive sources and methods.

Increasingly, however, centres could rely exclusively on open sources, assisted by advanced processing and knowledge management techniques. They would be able to produce unclassified intelligence on military deployments, doctrines and budgets, for example, that would underpin global or regional CSBMs and arms control regimes. As important, staff seconded to such centres would have the opportunity both to work with erstwhile enemies in a relatively open atmosphere and to achieve a common understanding of their operational environment.

Third, and perhaps most significantly, the information revolution could transform the role of outside parties in verifying the implementation of peace accords, and, in some respects, arms control regimes. Generally, peace agreements have been verified by states parties, often with the help of a small number of outside countries, notably the US. This was the case, for instance, with the Israel– Egypt Separation of Forces Agreement of January 1974. With global arms control measures, such as the 1968 Nuclear Non-Proliferation Treaty (NPT), it has also been certain leading states that have sometimes supported verification with national intelligence.

Overwhelmingly, the international community has relied on the US— the only country with the global monitoring resources needed for the job. The information revolution changes this situation. While the American intelligence community will continue to have capabilities unmatched by other states or by the commercial sector, an increasing number of verification tasks can be carried out using open sources and methods. Consequently, the capability to assess agreements is proliferating along with the technology.

Since 1995, the Western European Union (EU) has operated a satellite centre that primarily uses CSI to assist with monitoring the 1990 Conventional Armed Forces in Europe (CFE) Treaty.

The IAEA is beginning to fuse a range of open sources to enable it to detect proactively violations of the NPT Research centres are showing an increasing capability to track weapons of mass destruction (WMD) developments across the world, and NGOs, such as the transnational Forum on Early Warning and Response, are exploiting open sources and communication networks to help predict humanitarian crises. And companies like the US-based Open Source Solutions and Stratfor offer a routine political and military monitoring service.

The result is that future arms control and CSBM regimes will be able to call on a much wider range of outside parties to assist with verification. The US will still have a role to play, but agencies like the IAEA and the Organization for the Prohibition of Chemical Weapons (OPCW) will be able to do much more themselves. In addition, other state actors, non-state actors (like research institutes and activist networks), companies and media outlets will be able to contribute to verification.

### *Challenges*

The information revolution not only makes verification easier, but, in certain respects, it poses new problems. Three of the most significant are:

- encryption;
- technology diffusion; and
- electronic attack capabilities.

The debate over encryption policy is a well-worn one in Western societies. Towards the end of 1999 the US government seemed to have acknowledged that it was fighting a losing battle in seeking to control the export of encryption software. Its more liberal approach parallels that of other states. Nonetheless Western intelligence agencies are still grappling with the likely loss of one of their most useful sources: signals intelligence from intercepted communications.

Encryption poses a similar problem for CBSMs and arms control verification. Western intelligence agencies that help to monitor such regimes rely heavily on SIGINT, tapping into global civilian, military and government voice and data links.

Although they have the computing power to crack most encryption codes in time, the widespread availability of encryption to governments, citizens and sub-state groups will make their job much harder, more time consuming and more resource intensive. The proliferation of strong encryption thus makes it harder for national signals intelligence agencies to assist with verification.

Another concern is that small states and sub-state groups may exploit freely available commercial information and communication technologies in order to utilise limited resources against their larger opponents. These technologies range from mobile, secure, satellite communications, through intelligence gathering and mission planning tools, to precision-guided munitions.

If networked, media-savvy groups or state organisations take advantage of this combination of technologies they could pose serious military threats to status quo powers. Russia has faced a precursor to this problem with the Chechen rebels, and the US with Osama bin Laden. In verification terms, this raises difficult questions about the nature of dual-use technologies and the convergence of military and civilian technologies and applications.

These difficulties are brought into sharp focus in the emerging debate over information warfare (IW). This is a broad concept, but a particularly problematic aspect is that of electronic attack or, more specifically, Computer Network Attack (CNA).

The latter involves the use of computers to launch a logical strike on terminals via digital networks and telecommunication links. Assaults may result in the denial of services or the compromising of data integrity and confidentiality. Although long used as a tool of espionage and to some extent integrated into battlefield electronic warfare, CNA is becoming of greater concern to countries and businesses that are ever more reliant on networked information systems and the Internet.

A number of states have followed the US lead in identifying logical threats to their increasingly interconnected and interdependent Critical National Infrastructure (CNI) as major security concerns. These fears have led to a debate over how best to characterise and deal with the danger. The approach currently favoured by the US and its allies, which are investing in offensive IW techniques, is to treat it as a criminal or terrorist problem. They are pushing for enhanced international co-operation in order to put in place the legal, technical and policing measures necessary to ensure that all countries work together to protect their CNI and the global information infrastructure.

An opposite perspective has emerged from states that feel threatened by the possibility of offensive CNA by the West. Russia has championed this approach and has proposed that the UN treats IW as a military issue in the General Assembly's First Committee and discusses outlawing it. This involves viewing CNA as military technology, and thus devising laws of armed conflict and, possibly, arms control measures to restrict its proliferation and use. There is growing pressure from within Western millilitres to exploit their advantages in this field. This is likely to energise other members of the international community to push for controls and to consider ways of limiting this new capability. Paradoxically, the problem is that any conceivable regime to restrict the use or possession of IW poses tremendous challenges for verification.

## Regulating Media Revolution

Within the last forty years, as television has come to dominate our cultural life, television (and radio) broadcasting in Britain has moved from a position of a BBC monopoly to the doorstep of a new era of virtually unlimited channels, high quality picture and sound and the availability of interactive services through the convergence of broadcasting, telecommunications and computer facilities.

At the same time, arguably, an obvious potential for domination of this brave new world by unaccountable and unashamedly commercial international conglomerates has developed. The position and role of regulators has come under increasing scrutiny and strain over this period, and especially over the last fifteen years or so, as the pace of change has increased.

Meanwhile, reactive regulatory reform has resulted in a curious mix of structural, behavioural and content-specific regulation which will often pull regulators in different directions, and can easily obscure regulatory objectives. The fundamental rationales for, and objectives of, regulation stand in desperate need of reappraisal, and new, or at least radically reconstructed versions of old concepts must be developed if regulatory approaches are to be relevant to the changed and still-changing media environment.

That the media is going through a period of revolution is a truism. The degree of change, in terms of both technological convergence between media and the globalisation of media markets, is massive and far-reaching, and far from completed. The potential for 'interactive television', especially through broad-band cable technology allowing the combination of conventional and interactive television with computer network and telecommunications facilities, demonstrates the need for a regulatory regime based on new foundations.

If concrete evidence of convergence is needed, Marsden (1997) provides it when he refers us to an attempt by Microsoft, Intel and Compaq to set PC-dominated standards for digital television, an event which he describes as 'a watershed in the convergence of computing and telecommunications'. The latest relevant British legislation, the Broadcasting Act 1996, can best be viewed as a holding operation, and in the medium-term, steps such as splitting responsibility for the regulation of digital terrestrial television (DTT) between the ITC and Oftel, seem just as likely to create confusion and uncertainty as consistent, effective regulation.

The nature and degree of the media revolution is such that ad hoc, incremental and often reactive change in light of new circumstances will not be sufficient, yet as Humphreys notes in his study of mass media policy in Western Europe, 'Increasingly, public policies have tended to follow technological and market developments'. If media regulation is to achieve anything meaningful, what is needed as a matter of urgency is a more fundamental review of the rationales, techniques and consequences relating to media regulation, that can lay a sound foundation for responses to ongoing and future developments.

In Oftel's terms, what is needed is 'a systematic effort to ensure consistency of approach to the regulation of communications networks, whether these are wire or fibre-based or wireless, or broadcast or hybrids of these'. However, the challenges to media regulation do not arise solely out of technological developments. Changes of corporate structure in the media market have produced, for example, the domination of conventional commercial broadcasting in Italy by Berlusconi and the domination of the British press by two news groups, demonstrating the need for reappraisal of the regulatory regime if pluralism is to be maintained.

As Bagdikian summarises the issue, 'If a small number of publishers, all with the same special outlook, dominate the marketplace of public ideas, something vital is lost to an open society'. The kind of international cross-media empire developed by Murdoch, or the dominance of Canal+ and Kirch on mainland Europe, poses a further clear threat to pluralism, but cannot properly be addressed either on a sectoral basis or within individual legal jurisdictions.

Over-spill of broadcasting, across national borders, presents one obvious practical problem for national regulators concerned, for example, with the control of violent or sexually explicit imagery. Collins and Murroni refer to this phenomenon, succinctly as 'the erosion of national communications sovereignty through technological change'.

While the global nature of the Internet presents a particular set of international problems, the US Supreme Court's recent decision regarding the Communications Decency Act 1996 demonstrates the difficulties of legislating on such matters even in a domestic setting. The maintenance of plurality within a domestic market also becomes more difficult, if not impossible, when ownership is contained within a series of international media conglomerates which may have little in the way of meaningful national affiliations.

From the perspective of ensuring competition, national efforts to limit the growth of cross-media empires may be undermined by the perceived national economic interest in allowing such conglomerates to grow large if they are to compete effectively on the international arena. To quote Bagdikian again, 'some national governments encourage formation of dominant national firms so that they can better compete in a world-wide race'.

These outcomes of the media revolution appear to demand a root and branch review of regulatory policy and practice, yet to date we have seen only marginal changes. Proposals for a single media or communications regulator appear to be gathering momentum, and international, especially European, organisations play an increasingly significant part in media regulation.

The electronic programme guides and conditional access systems (CASs) required for the viewer to receive

DTT, form new pinch-points in the commercial television market, with control of these gateways permitting the possibility of domination of the market by one player. BSkyB, is already the virtual monopoly player in British satellite television, and is part of Rupert Murdoch's News Corporation group that controls over 35 per cent of the British national press. This group also looks likely to be first in the field with DTT decoders, and, as the probable key supplier of major programming to DTT has the potential to develop rapidly a monopoly power over this new market.

Under the new structure created by the Broadcasting Act 1996, and, the Advanced Television Services Regulations 1996 which implements EC Directive 95/47 (Advanced Television Standards Directive), the telecommunications regulator, Oftel, has now been given a key role in licensing the decoder systems (CASs) which will be necessary in order to receive DTT, and in establishing guidelines for the CAS sector.

Oftel's brief extends also to the more general objective of avoiding the risks of abuse of dominant positions within new markets, and it can be argued that this role will be crucial if widespread benefit is to accrue from the advent of the digital era. In June 1997, despite acknowledging the qualities of a competing bid from Digital Television Network (DTN), the ITC awarded control (ITC, 1997) of the three commercial multiplexes for DTT to the British Digital Broadcasting (BDB) consortium.

However, influenced in part, no doubt by advice from Oftel, the ITC was only prepared to accept the BDB bid if BSkyB were to sell its one-third equity holding to the other consortium members, Granada and Carlton. The losing bidder for the multiplexes, DTN, was reported as considering an application for judicial review in relation to the licence award, however, precedent suggests that such a step would be more related to publicity than anything else, given the courts' track-record of reluctance in overturning ITC licence allocation decisions.

Evidence in this field suggests that the British courts cannot necessarily be relied upon to ensure rationality or even transparency in the exercise of the power such as the award of licences to broadcasters. It can be argued that British courts, basing their actions to a large extent upon the limited concept of 'Wednesbury reasonableness', do not apply the same, rigorous standards of review as do, for example, their US counterparts.

This example demonstrates the fact that the kind of reactive and marginal reform of the British media regulation regime brought about in recent years has failed to resolve tensions between competing regulatory approaches and philosophies. Indeed, in confirming attempts to allow the co-existence of competing and potentially conflicting rationales, it indicates a degree of complacency and myopia which is likely to prove dangerous in the context of the ongoing media revolution.

A degree of tension between regulators sharing jurisdiction is inevitable, and perhaps even helpful in the short term if it facilitates the articulation of clear regulatory standards. However, in the longer term it might be expected to result primarily in uncertainty, and may impede the identification and attainment of regulatory goals.

The issues raised for the public lawyer in the context of media regulation are both widespread and obvious.

Extending beyond the intricacies of individual court decisions in judicial review cases involving regulatory bodies, the network of, often interrelating and overlapping regulatory institutions and the role of government in relation to them, and, the existence of both statutory and non-statutory regimes all provide obvious focal points.

We can also readily identify problems arising out of the different approaches which are likely to be adopted by national and international bodies which may approach issues from different jurisprudential, constitutional and economic perspectives. It is therefore surprising to find that while adequate legal commentaries are readily available, surprisingly little analysis has been carried out by public lawyers, in the UK at least.

There are honourable exceptions to this: in the past, Norman D. Lewis and Mike Elliott have identified and focused upon aspects of this agenda, and Tom Gibbons has taken the time and trouble to pursue a more wide-ranging analysis, though this work has now been largely overtaken by events. More recently still, Lesley Hitchens has made a significant contribution in scrutinising recent developments and indicating the need for a more thorough and considered policy review.

However, the net effect of these contributions, while enlightening in many ways, is to leave largely untouched the underlying issues, focusing as they do primarily upon specific developments and occurrences rather than the broader issues and rationales which underlie the subject. Put more specifically, rather like the activities of government and the media regulators, the focus of commentators has tended to be on amendments to the institutional structure and the outcomes of regulation and its reform rather than upon the rationales for the regulatory endeavour.

Such tinkering with the fine detail is unlikely to equip us adequately to address the challenges posed by the ongoing media revolution. It seems largely futile to examine regulatory policies, mechanisms and outcomes without first reflecting upon the objectives, deriving from principles, in turn born of the rationales for intervention.

The range of rationales in play suggest a significant role for the media specialist, the political scientist, economist, sociologist and many others, but the lawyer, arguably, must justify their interest. Conventional British legal academics have done little more than to catalogue or chronicle the legal rules in play, however, a wider view of law can be applied.

While public lawyers clearly have an interest in the administrative law and practice applicable to an area such as media regulation, they must also place this in its constitutional context, and scrutinise legitimacy and rationality as well as mere legality. Such an approach demands not only the examination of technical rules, but also their relationship to fundamental constitutional and democratic values.

A conventional public law analysis of the institutions of media regulation can offer much, both in terms of substantive and procedural comment. However, there is a sense in which such critique becomes vacuous if not integrated with an understanding of the values which inform any such regime. At the heart of liberal-democratic theory is a concept of citizenship.

If citizenship implies effective participation in society, it can be argued that in an era where effective participation has come to rely increasingly upon access to the media as the primary arena for political and cultural communication, access to the media has itself become a prerequisite of effective citizenship. 'Access', in this context, clearly implies the ability to receive media output, but also, arguably, implies an ability to input to the media and influence the agenda.

The access to the media in terms of receiving media output, the public lawyer, in addition to considering the nature of rules and norms existing in this field, and the quality of the administrative process, must also recognise that access to the media should be utilised as a yardstick when examining existing and proposed regulatory mechanisms. In the absence of adequate clarity regarding the rationales and objectives of regulation, it is unlikely that we can analyse meaningfully the policies, mechanisms and results of regulation.

A potentially bewildering array of regulatory techniques have grown up in Britain and comparable jurisdictions, ranging from statutory to self-regulatory methods, and based at both national and international levels. These various approaches can be divided further into general and media-specific competition measures, and those focused on form (or structure of ownership) and effects (or behaviour and its consequences) within media markets.

Specific regulatory frameworks may exist not only in relation to ownership and licensing of broadcasting or print-media corporations, but also in relation to content or output. Increasingly, regulatory attention must turn also to delivery mechanisms, and CASs and the like. Often, specific techniques have been developed in relation to particular sectors of the media, but modern developments require a global view on a cross-media basis cutting across conventional sectoral divides.

Acknowledgement of the convergence of telecommunications and broadcasting media can be seen to be implicitly acknowledged in the overlapping roles of the ITC and Oftel in relation to licensing and regulation of the CAS arrangements for DTT, yet this must be viewed simply as one more incremental change, rather than the radical overhaul of the regulatory regime that is indicated.

Marsden suggests that regulation for competition between platforms (DTT, direct-to-home (DTH) satellite, and cable) must be the key for telecommunications liberalisation. Though delivery of television by cable in Britain remains far below the levels achieved in mainland Europe, DTH satellite broadcasting provides an obvious source of competition to DTT, though is itself dominated by BSkyB.

Ensuring the existence of a range of platforms would, however, require a high degree of structural regulation, and arguably a degree of intervention which no British government would be likely to support. Indeed, though committed to the activities of market forces in relation to the media, preferring largely, for example, to allow an industry standard for CASs to emerge rather than imposing one, all government (both Conservative and Labour) rhetoric and legislative activity in the last two years has supported the development of DTT, for example by seeking to ensure quality and attractiveness of product by guaranteeing space on the multiplexes for the conventional, terrestrial, public service broadcasters.

In so far as a common thread can be discerned running through the regulatory arrangements, this thread can be identified as market-oriented. In Britain, and other countries in which current perceptions of democracy tend to push governments away from direct intervention in media output, regulation of ownership, in the name of market competition, has become a significant means of seeking to achieve desired outcomes.

General competition law provisions provide the background here though differences in emphasis between different regimes should be noted. In Britain, investigations into mergers and take-overs will normally be triggered by the acquisition taking a holding beyond a stated limit within a market (form-based competition regulation) while within the EU, the emphasis is on effects rather than form, based on the provisions of Articles 85 and 86 which seek to prohibit restriction or distortion of competition or abuse of a dominant position within a market.

However, in addition to general competition law provisions, media specific measures seek to establish limits on ownership and control of enterprises either within or across media sectors. These range from the provisions of the Fair Trading Act 1973, which allows wide discretion to the Secretary of State in regulating control of newspaper take-overs and mergers, to the complex provisions on cross-media ownership contained in the Broadcasting Act 1996.

The overall objective here would appear to be diversity of output, though the regulatory focus is clearly on ownership. There is a real sense in which the focus on competition via control of ownership can be viewed as surrogate for regulation for plurality in output. This option is obviously tempting given that, though by no means easy, and subject to varying methods of calculation, it is somewhat easier to measure and impose limits on ownership than to determine and define requirements of diversity in output.

However, the emphasis on competition law, both general and media-specific measures, as the primary mechanism of ensuring plurality in the media can be questioned, a number of commentators having identified the underlying problem. Humphreys states that '. . . one of the main challenges for the future will be to keep the media diverse and pluralistic in the face of powerful pressures towards economic concentration'.

Meanwhile, Beltrame correctly identifies the extent to which competition law can be seen as too blunt an instrument to ensure the desired diversity of output, noting that the European Commission 'argues that the objectives of competition law and those of media ownership laws are profoundly different, in that mergers which, economically speaking do not threaten competition, might well suffocate plurality of media'.

The fact that the media supplies and influences our view of the world, and has become the primary means for civic, political and cultural communication, demands a degree of equality of access to the media's output if equality of citizenship is acknowledged as a legitimate objective. However, it is the perceived benefits of market competition that underlie the basic framework of competition law, and also drove the British government to take a passive attitude towards the development of CAS equipment, preferring to allow a market driven standard to emerge.

European moves towards regulation via structural separation of programming from carriage are premised on consumer benefit which will arise from markets being liberalised and gateways kept open or opened. However, Harcourt notes that despite repeated pressure from the European Parliament, moves towards EU measures on media concentration have been delayed by the nature of the institutional dynamics within and between the Directorates General of the Commission, and political tensions between Member States, indicating the risk of institutional inertia arising in the absence of an appropriate regulatory framework being established.

Marsden also correctly draws attention to the problems raised for regulators operating within different regulatory traditions. In liberalised and privatised telecommunications markets such as Britain, telecommunications have largely been regulated by reference to behavioural standards, while regulation of television has largely continued to be carried out on a structural basis, the emphasis being very much on ownership, though with the addition of industry-specific behavioural controls in the form of regulation of content.

Where regulators operating from different traditions are called to act together, tensions will be inevitable. Marsden seems to indicate the likelihood of the 'turf war' between the ITC and Oftel over regulation of CASs being decided in Oftel's favour, with the resulting probability of behavioural regulation predominating. This, it can be argued, would be fundamentally unsatisfactory, at least if behavioural regulation became the predominant or single track approach.

It is true to suggest that, ultimately, behavioural regulation in relation to specific pinch-points addresses directly the perceived problems of competition within the market, but, such regulation cannot operate effectively alone. It depends for its effectiveness upon the existence of a genuinely competitive market environment beyond specific bottlenecks which in itself, arguably, requires structural regulation.

Anti-competitive behaviour at particular pinch-points will be influenced and shaped by pressures arising from activities in the broader field, and attempts to regulate behaviour, say, in relation to CASs for DTT, will be doomed to failure if the entire environment in which DTT operates is ultimately shaped by the structure of the broader media industry beyond the DTT marketplace.

Such an institutional structure must draw on aspects of both structural and behavioural regulation (considering both the corporate structure of media conglomerates and their share of markets, but also, how dominant positions are actually used in relation to competition) but before it can carry out such a task effectively, meaningful objectives must be determined from more clearly articulated rationales for intervention.

In part, any mismatch between regulatory mechanisms and outcomes on the one hand and regulatory values and objectives on the other may be explained by virtue of the clear inconsistencies and conflicts discernible both within and between the various justifications for media regulation. In particular, the conflict between economies of scale, and perceived national interests in the development of large domestic media corporations must be set against the claimed benefits of pluralism and diversity.

The failure to develop a rational basis for the resolution of this conflict may be considered to be the most obvious cause of inconsistent and unsatisfactory regulation under existing and past arrangements. However, it can be argued that the greater degree of lack of achievement in regulation arises simply out of inadequate consideration of the fundamental, underlying values.

Such lack of reflection on fundamentals, and the failure to articulate objectives with reasonable clarity goes some way towards explaining the generally reactive nature of regulatory change noted by Elliott over fifteen years ago. The apparent objectives of regulation vary between prevention of monopoly (or abuse of monopolistic/monopsonistic/oligopolistic power), the protection of differing versions of 'public service' values, and the provision of choice, in terms of product, political viewpoint, and cultural diversity.

Arguably, the debate over objectives has increasingly been focused on consumer choice of media product, at the expense of broader, citizen oriented, expectations such as those underlying the public service tradition in broadcasting or the imposition of Universal Service Obligations (USOs) in relation to utilities.

Emphasising consumer choice, apparently as an end in itself, avoids the establishment of policy preferences in terms of specific, substantive outcomes or objectives. This produces not only an undue emphasis on (a version of) one rationale for regulatory intervention, but also, by allowing consumer choice to determine the ultimate shape of the media market, creates a high degree of uncertainty.

For example, it is unclear whether, in an open market, the consumer would ultimately be tempted most by the charms of DTT, or satellite services, or broad-band cable facilities. Traders in each will be plying their wares, but ultimately this may result in an undesirable trade war, replicating in a new forum the kind of battle of formats between VHS and Betamax in the home video market which resulted in so much consumer dissatisfaction before VHS finally won-out.

The address to the Royal Television Society in September 1997 by Chris Smith, Secretary of State for Culture, Media and Sport confirmed that the present government is following the lead of its predecessor, in facilitating the development of DTT. However, it is by no means certain that this is what the consumer market would or will prefer.

If serious about the creation of market choice, a government may find itself with no logical alternative to regulating for a range of acceptable, alternative delivery platforms though even this must be carried out in such a way as to integrate the regulation of control of platforms alongside transmission, production and CASs as part of the broadcasting market as a whole.

It is probably correct for the regulatory emphasis to shift increasingly towards delivery mechanisms, however, when focusing on this particular area, the regime must remain aware of the broader market context in which delivery mechanisms exist, and be informed by clear objectives, arising out of clearly defined rationales for intervention.

To intervene is not to deny market forces, but to give effect to them. Almost nowhere does a market survive which is not regulated, and in an area such as the media, which shows such clear tendencies towards monopoly, regulation is the necessary partner of market forces if the perceived benefits of the market are to accrue.

Ultimately, a consistent and effective regime of regulation can only exist where the justification for regulation is articulated with reasonable clarity, and in this respect difficult choices must be made between competing and often conflicting rationales. It is this area of the debate where failure to date has been the greatest.

Justifications for regulating the media can, broadly, be broken-down into three or four groups. The first relates to effectiveness of communication. In the context of the broadcast media, a particular related version of this argument has been that effective broadcast communication of necessity required regulation of broadcasting, as a result of the need to allocate and separate frequencies to avoid intermodulation (cross-channel interference).

While of some strength historically, this argument is about to lose all currency in the context of the vast, almost infinite, expansion of channels available as a result of digital and satellite technology. The second group of arguments for regulating the media derive from arguments which can, again, be broadly classified as pluralist.

Thus, arising from an acknowledgement of the power of the media, we find, in the liberal-democratic context, arguments for diversity of ownership, with the aim of ensuring the circulation of a range of views: cultural and political diversity. On occasion, such arguments can be amended significantly to provide a cultural-protectionist version.

The protection of minority languages such as Dutch, or even major languages such as French, against the cultural imperialism of a (US) English dominated world media can be conceived as an argument for cultural and linguistic diversity on the global scale.

These first two rationales for regulation seem to derive from rationales for freedom of expression based on arguments from truth, self-fulfilment or citizen participation though both are clearly premised on the perceived liberal-democratic ideal of the ability of all to have access to the 'market-place of ideas'.

Running parallel to this is a third, economics based, argument, that monopoly, and even possibly oligopoly, is undesirable as it denies the perceived benefits that are said to derive from the operation of an effective market. Deriving from the second argument's concern with plurality of media material, and potentially (though not necessarily) cutting across the third of avoidance of monopoly, is a fourth line of argument.

This concerns a public service ethos, which though encapsulated in Britain by Reith's tripartite typology of 'informing, educating and entertaining' will be interpreted differently in different countries. While regulation with a sole objective of preserving public service values may inhibit market developments, and may indeed ultimately stifle plurality of media product, the public service rationale for media regulation is said to derive from a desire to ensure the availability of a range of quality products, especially in relation to the media's role of enhancing the viewer's or reader's view of the world.

The public service approach is related to the 'social responsibility' model identified by Siebert et al, acknowledging the crucial role played by the media in equipping individual citizens for participation in society, while also acknowledging that the media is hugely significant in terms of providing 'a cultural cohesion to the nation'.

All of these various rationales for regulating the media must be considered when regulatory reform is broached. It is only rarely, however, that the competing rationales can be or will be neatly separated. Rather, they will often be melded together and encapsulated in what can prove to be a singularly unhelpful term: 'the public interest'.

Whenever this term appears it requires the closest possible scrutiny, as it invariably comprises a portmanteau, the contents of which must be examined closely. Sometimes, it will contain a meaning approximating to one of the rationales set-out above, sometimes more than one, sometimes all four in some combination.

The tension and conflict between these competing public interest claims is obvious. The regulators will have to balance potential economic benefits against the values of plurality and diversity and the effects on competition. This leaves the regulators with an unenviable task, akin to comparing apples with oranges, and, in the British context, we cannot be sure that any such decision will be taken via a transparent process, or even that adequate reasons will be given or required to enable us to check the rationality of such decision-making.

Thus, the absence of a meaningful construct of 'public interest' not only permits, if not encourages, inconsistency in regulation, but also hands to regulators significant, and largely unchecked, discretionary power. Underlying various rationales for regulation are differing versions of arguments relating to freedom of effective expression, dependant increasingly upon access to the media

The approaches adopted often take on board arguments relating to diversity in media products, both in political and cultural terms, but will also often be influenced also by economic, market-driven arguments, and may also seek to perpetuate public service values. It is argued that all of these approaches are, within the context of liberal-democracies, premised upon expectations of citizenship, and that effective access to the media (in terms of both input and output) is in effect a prerequisite of effective citizenship.

With this in mind, to place citizenship at the heart of any meaningful concept of 'the public interest' would seem to be a logical necessity. The move away from a world of five analogue, terrestrial television channels to a new era of interactive television integrated with wider computer and telecommunications facilities, accessible in many cases via costly gateway facilities, presents the risk of heightened social division; an increase in the hierarchy of information 'haves' and 'have nots' and therefore heightened social inequality.

Given the necessity of media access for effective citizenship, it seems reasonable to privilege equality of citizenship as the key rationale for media regulation. At the most general level, Collins and Murroni state that 'What is needed is competition policy where competition can thrive in the public interest and regulation where it cannot'. In itself, this seems perfectly reasonable, though ultimately is heavily dependant upon an adequately developed and transparent concept of 'the public interest'.

In an era in which market-based philosophy enjoys a virtually unchallenged hegemonic position, it is difficult for a government to take so unfashionable a position as to limit the influence of market forces by reference to other, arguably higher, values. However, for a government said to value citizenship and community, taking steps to ensure social inclusion and equality of citizenship would be perfectly consistent.

In a sense, therefore, unfashionably, Collins and Murroni advocate the active exercise of policy-making power, and also regulatory power, in the public interest. This active, policy-making role is unfashionable in the sense that hands-off government, and liberalisation or de-regulation, is the dominant philosophy in

The major problem is the identification and articulation of regulatory objectives, often masked by the use of the nebulous 'public interest'. The common thread underlying the public interest claims in relation to media regulation can best be described as feeding into the broader constitutional endeavour of effective citizen participation. Effective participation can be equated with informed participation, and this in turn requires a diverse range of views to be in circulation and accessible to as wide a range of the population as possible in order to allow for comparison and triangulation.

Concentration in media markets, though not necessarily contrary to diversity of content, tends to have a strong contingent effect of limiting the range of views available for scrutiny. This effect can already be readily observed in the British newspaper sector, and now, with increasing dependence upon new technology to access broadcast information and computer information resources, both at a price, concentration presents a dual threat of risking further concentration in relation to technological gateways and simultaneously creating a two-tier information society.

# 2

# ICTs in Mass Communication

The overwhelming impact and the information society that this computer generated network has seemed to generate against the backdrop of class disparities and market economy and the widening gap between information have and have-nots. The essay focuses on the concept of 'Information' and how it becomes a commodity and a tool in the context of new information economy.

A theoretical structure of the evolution of new communication technologies and its outcome in developing different interest groups in terms of access and privileges, have been outlined. As a result of this, two controversial schools of thoughts have emerged which in turn put an effect in analyzing the outcomes.

These trends at the one hand, focused on the overwhelming and trouble-shooting nature of the technology which has been thought to be driven by market forces and on the other hand, emphasized on the existing disparities that has been widened by the advent of ICTs.

An argument that the market forces alone will not ratify this structure of information disparities has also been discussed. The essay urged the need of an alternative information source where these issues could have been critically analyzed and could be discussed with the idea of an equal perspective. Accordingly, a website and a CD ROM for an alternative information source has been recommended to develop.

A media grown global middle class might weave for an 'Information Superhighway', might consider cyberspace as to be altering every sphere of their lives but it also has got little relevance to the majority of the world where even intermediate technologies are underdeveloped. The shape of Information Technology revolution has been developed by the logic and interests of advanced capitalism, without being reducible to the expressions of such interests.

In this economy as we can functionally observe the productivity and competitiveness of units and agents depends heavily on the capacity to generate, process and to apply efficiently knowledge based information. The emergence of a new technological paradigm organized around new, more powerful, and more flexible information technologies makes it possible for information itself to become the product of the production process.

It means information is becoming an object in terms of its production and distribution and thus establishes the very essence of Information Theory. The current process of technological transformation expands exponentially because of its ability to create an interface between technological fields through common digital language in which information is generated, stored, retrieved, processed and transmitted.

Information theory commodities information, draining it of semantic content. Encoded electronically and treated as being without meaning, messages became far more malleable than they were traditionally. The theory is based on Norbert Wiener's famous book - "Cybernetics: or Control and Communication in the Animal and the Machine" which was published in 1961.

The concept of Information society has also been supported in some other earlier work of few social scientists such as Daniel Bell, Alain Touraine, Tom Stonier, Alvin Toffler etc. "They all share the notion that Society is being transformed by a revolution in information technology, which is creating an entirely new social structure. Such advocates suggest that, we are witnessing the demise of the industrial age with the replacement of capital and labour as the chief resources of economic growth by information and knowledge as the primary means of development".

In this dissertation we would look at different perceptions of Information and Communication revolution and would critically evaluate the impact, controversies and values of this information society within the paradigm of media, society and development. As an extension of this dissertation my final project will be to experiment with an alternative information source (New Internationalists) both in online (website) and offline (CD ROM) digital mode.

Internet emerges in the US as a species of spin-off from a national security project rather any sort of discrete 'invention'. But its also true that BBN team left the main frame programmers free to deal with a number of issues, the protocols for incoming data for example, has been one of these.

Very rapidly the mainframe teams formed themselves into a Network Working Group (NWG) which established the prompt system, now used for log-in name and password, by creating the L-O-G-I-N command, Host-to-host protocols, Telnet, Network Control Protocol (NCP), File Transfer Protocol (FTP) etc.

Today's Internet grows out of ARPANET, which was based on PDP8, and PDP11 computers located in American Universities that were all linked by permanently open telephone lines. Originally used to facilitate communications between the military and academic researchers working on military contracts, ARPANET underwent a major reorganization in 1983 and it split into military and civilian sections.

The Internet is basically a direct outcome of the civilian section of ARPANET which recommended for IP and IP was adopted by academic and government organizations as a means of exchanging information between their mainframe computers and also as a method of scholarly communication using electronic mail. Gradually all other LAN in the world adopted IP.

While this evolution was on, some other ideas and technologies, such as, queuing theory, packet switching and electronic mail etc. also added a valuable component to the improved utility of the electronic networking jigsaw. In those early days academics used the new network for electronic mail, bulletin boards, news groups, sharing software and drawing down large fields of statistical information.

Commercial part of the Internet actually began in 1989 when Compuserve a US company previously concerned with providing data bank services, began to offer full Internet access to subscribers wishing to use e-mail. CompuServe services were followed in 1993 by America Online Ltd. and Delphi who offered access to data banks, electronic mail, as well as online chat services.

These service providers also permitted their subscribers to receive and send software and computer file using the file transfer protocol (ftp), as well as use remote computers interactively. But this computer mediated network reached a dramatic turn when optic fiber cable took the medium of transmission as it transmits photons (i.e. light) where cable or telephone wires transmit electrons (i.e electricity).

Optical technologies promise a greater expansion in the bandwidth of the telecommunication network. Optic fiber cables are hair thin strands of pure, highly transparent glass through which pulses of light from a LASER are transmitted. The electronic signal is encoded digitally and then converted into pulses of laser light by an 'emitter' which are then transmitted down the fiber to an optical detector which converts them back to electronic form.

As Ben Bagdikian and others have noted in studies of the global media empires, very few private transnational corporations (TNCs) dominate the news, information, ideas, entertainment and popular culture that most people in the world receive. Huge corporations are controlling ever-growing shares of the global market.

By the late 1990s one fifth of world population living in the high-income countries had at their disposal 74 percent of telephone lines, and accounted for over 93 percent of Internet users. According to 1998 UNDP Human Development report, 18.5% of the world population have a radio, 14.5% have a television, 0.4%

have a telephone line, 0.7% have a computer and 0.05% have Internet access.

Tele-density in many African countries is less than 0.5 per 100 inhabitants, says a March 1999 ITU report. In India it is 1.86 lines per 100 persons, compared to over 60 per 100 inhabitants in the United states and Canada. Says the Human Development Report 1997.

Internet is growing at exponential rates but is overwhelmingly located in the already industrialized world where users are wealthy, white and highly educated. Representation of women on the Internet varies significantly. Though it has witnessed a slower growth of users online over the years still the women in the South are significantly left out.

An approximation to the evolving architecture of information flows in the global economy shows the hierarchy of information being transmitted from United States to most of the developed and industrialized countries of the world. Even within the developed countries and societies the IT penetration and access to telecommunication facilities are not equal. Computer ownership patterns even in USA correlate strongly with age and income.

In the U.S., the professional and middle classes have found the Internet to be useful for communication with some government agencies, for some forms of shopping, for tackling investments, maintaining ties with friends and family via email, and as a source of entertainment. There are also many examples where the Internet enables the middle class public to have better access to important information.

From all these illustrated points one thing is clear that only the rich, powerful, elite and middle-class within the societies are connected and would be able to rip off the benefits of this technology while the rest is being dominated with the outcome of this information domination and will always be in technologically dependent economies.

## Ownership pattern

Ownership pattern does not tell itself the social consequences of information revolution in its full-length as it is also important to understand some of the algorithms of this technological pattern that affects different sub-systems. What characterize the current technological revolution are not the centrality of knowledge and information, but the application of such knowledge and information to knowledge generation and information processing/communication devices, in a cumulative feedback loop between innovation and the uses of innovation.

The uses of new communication technologies in the past two decades have gone through three distinct stages.

(1) The automation of tasks

(2) An experimentation of uses

(3) A reconfiguration of applications.

In the first two stages, technological innovation progressed through learning by using, while in the third stage, the users learned technology by doing and reconfiguring the networks and finding new applications. The feedback loop between introducing new technology, using it and developing it into new realms becomes much faster under the new technological paradigm.

New information technologies are not simply tools to be applied, but processes to be developed. Users and doers may become the same. Thus users can take control of technology as it happens for the Internet. This is an important point, as for the first time in the history, the human mind is a direct productive force, not just a decisive element of the production system. It might put the peripheral and underdeveloped economies in a position where they can reverse the trend against the monopolies.

But that might not be as easy as we are writing about and the interests of global trade usually act against this process. Global economy is politically constituted. Restructuring of business firms and new information technologies, while being at the source of globalization trends, could not have evolved, without the policies of de-regulations, privatization and liberalization of trade and investment. And these policies were decided and enacted by the industrialized country's governments, multinationals and international economic institutions. They did so to preserve/enhance the interests of their states, within their given paradigm of values and priorities.

There are the lower strata of less affluent and mobile wage earners, who seem more likely to be, as Dordick et al put it, 'the information used'-experiencing different technological topologies. This consumer model of the Information Superhighway will have only limited capability for interactivity supporting the development of horizontal discourses.

As Calabrese and Borchert described "..wage earners, the precariously employed and the unemployed will interact infrequently on the horizontal dimension, except primarily in commercial modes which are institutionally and hierarchically structured and controlled for commercial purposes such as games and shopping and also do more routine forms of telework".

Finally, in the 'off-line' marginalised spaces there are disadvantaged groups living in poverty and structural unemployment who seem likely to be excluded altogether from electronic networks. Here, poverty and unemployment means that access to any electronic network or telecommunication facilities will be financially problematic. Access is denied in many cases as 'with technology and language both being owned by the wealthy, class divides are intrinsically linked to this hegemony'.

In analyzing the trends of social impacts of information technology, it is possible to be driven by a dilemma and the dilemma is of two controversial thoughts. One trend seems to be a bit euphoric and emphasizes the.benevolent and overwhelming nature of this technology as if the information and communication technology being a subversive tool itself will improve the socio-economic conditions if only some interventions can be made.

But the other trend focuses on the widening gap between information have and have-nots and how the existing social patterns continue to keep the socioeconomic disparities and/or work in favor of power and wealthy.

The dominating trend define the network as "Virtual societies" and "....are marked by political, technological and cultural pattern so intimately connected as to be nearly indistinguishable. ...For example, a virtual discussion may allow all to speak and all to be heard at once. Each participant types their contributions and places them in a centrally held discussion, accessible to all other participants....In this way all contributions are always available, no one can be silenced because their voice is the quietest and no one can be heard with more effect simply because they are more aggressive..Such distinctive forms of computer-mediated discussion give rise to the hope that, perhaps, virtual technology creates a more politically egalitarian debate.."

The rapid advancement of Information Technologies specially the development of the Internet, Email, Digital Television and Mobile Telèphony has created a sort of 'digital renaissance heralding a new information age in which individual tastes are catered for, citizens become better informed, and new wealth is created. But subscribers to this trend are actually fashionable to view Information Technology from individual perspective as Bill Gates wrote "The information highway is a tool of the individual" Prophets such as Peter Drucker, Alvin and Heidi Toffler, and Esther Dyson believe that the information revolution will make hierarchical bureaucracies obsolete and will lead to a new electronic feudalism with overlapping communities and jurisdictions to multiple layers of citizens' identities and loyalties.

Analyzing of impact according to this trend is more based on market forces and is somewhat thought that a combination of digital technology and free markets would bring rich and diverse media offerings to consumers which would lead to a boost of general economy. This optimism is actually rested on to a historical fact that deregulation and privatization of early 80s gave birth to the introduction of digital technologies in the 1990s. The rhetoric associated with these changes was that they would allow the fresh wind of competition to blow through the formerly monopolistic broadcasting and telecommunications industries.

According to this thought, a competitive market in digital media products will take the place of monopoly, precipitating 'de-massification of the media' in which 'the monolithic empires of mass media...dissolve into an array of cottage industries." Much of the current efforts to theorize democratic implications of new digital technologies rests on German philosopher Jurgen Habermas's concept of 'Public Sphere'. He argues that the development of early modern capitalism brought the concept of public property and reflected critical opinions in letters, novels, coffee.houses, salons etc. and helped emerging of an independent, market based press with critical judgment.

He saw the ideal Public Sphere as being space distinct from both the state and the market. But nevertheless Habermas's concept provides the theoretical backbone to thinking about the role of computer mediated communications in further democracy. Cyberspace enthusiasts suggest that, computer based network tends to bring back the Public Sphere concept which might be important for democratic discourse.

The current structure of the Internet still reflects its 'no central control' evolution with no one body owning or controlling the use of it. Something like a cross between the PC and citizens band radio its rules are made and policed by the users or, more precisely, by those users who are active enough to want to make rules and police them.

New users, particularly commercial users do not always find it easy to comprehend the decentralized, free wheeling and somewhat anarchic nature of the Internet. "The bigger players have the money, the clout, the physical strength and the social control to bludgeon their way through, but they do not have the flexibility, the ability to pop up and disappear at will, the speed of action or the elasticity to slip through the holes, that the well trained indivi dual has" over the Internet.

For theoreticians like Mark Poster Internet is important as a decentralize communication system, it can question the assumptions of older positions: "If the technological structure of the Internet institutes costless reproduction, instantaneous dissemination and radical decentralization, what might be its effects upon the society, the culture and the political institutions?"

Some characteristics of virtual communities like the one of Multi-user domain, games, news groups and other forms of networking can allow the participation of voices (such as minorities, women, greens etc.) who have been previously excluded. With the advent of new media technologies, audience segmentation and the advent of alternative political movements, Dahlgren see 'the contours of historically new conditions for the Public Sphere' emerging.

'The very sophistication of the information handling and processing options available to rich corporate environments, their ability to pay over the top for quite mediocre information solutions, and the strongly emerging imperative that all information should be regarded as a market driven commodity, has had a deleterious effect on current perceptions of publicly funded information.'

Thinkers like Neil Postman, Joseph Weizenbaum, Theodore Roszak and Frank Webster who believe that deployment of ICT will simply reinforce historical trends towards socioeconomic disparities, inequalities in political power and gaps between knowledge elite and the disenfranchised. Unafraid of being dubbed neo-Luddites, they predict massive job displacement and deskilling.

Between the two extremes is a small group of technorealists treading the middle ground "Although the information revolution could well exacerbate existing economic and cultural faultiness, thus widening the global rift between the North and the South, it also offers the possibility of a truly interconnected 'global village,' says Alan Hedley, the University of Victoria, Canada, sociologist, whose position is close to that of the technorealists.

The gap between technology "haves".and "have-nots" is unrelenting, says a US Department of Commerce report renewing concerns about how the info-chasm could contribute to economic injustice in the 21st century. The United States exports 120,000 hours of TV programming to Europe alone every year. The cola wars are fought on the Indian TV, celebrity cricketer and film stars backing one or the other cola. Music TV channels from the West have virtually destroyed interest in classical and native musical traditions among the youth even in countries like India which have well-developed and long-standing traditions.

US style junk food chain stores and branded clothes have invaded every country edging out less expensive and better suited local products. The age of political imperialism may be over, but cultural and economic imperialism is emerging with a vengeance. For the hitherto disenfranchised of the world, the new order could provide the means to organize and articulate their needs, such that they could eventually participate in a more just and humane, and hence sustainable world.

The Commodification of Public Sphere seems to be the major argument to establish the fact that this network though may be democratic or neutral in nature (like any other technological development) is not actually representing all classes and voices at the end. During the 1980s and 1990s the multimedia conglomerates passion for digital convergence has been encouraged by governments who saw market competition as the essential spur to the growth of the media and information industries.

The New Right rhetoric associated with building 'information superhighways' has stressed that only unrestrained market forces will build the infrastructure that is predicted to bring so many benefits to the general population. But in real world, increasing domination of capitalist global multimedia monopolies is taking away all the benefits that are being expected.

Even the free access culture is being motivated towards a business interest. Microsoft MSN services used to provide free distant calling in 1999 and 2000 but from the beginning of this year that started to put charges on it which is a common example of making people dependent on certain commodities and then to charge on these. However, even if access to cyberspace was more equitable it is not clear that this in itself would result in a more democratic and responsive political system since power does not depend on information alone.

The head of News Corporation, Rupert Murdoch, has often lauded the new media technologies as having the potential to empower people from the once powerful press barons. Yet, when the Chinese government objected to the BBCs coverage of their brutal suppression of pro-democracy protests, Murdoch did not hesitate to remove the BBC World service from his Star satellite, a move seemingly designed to placate a government with which he hoped to do business." Where information is power, denying information to marginalized communities, actively prevents the rural poor from overcoming the unequal power structures that they are trapped within.

While it is in the interest of the powerful in society to restrict such access, it is also in the interest of the powerful nations to deny access and maintain domination. The unrestricted flow of general information is an essential prerequisite for an egalitarian society.

In shor, media (Internet and all) is bombarding information, acceptance and denial both are projected and "cultures dominate by creating norms that are not questioned by creating 'accepted practices' that become tools of oppression and by defusing the need for critical analysis.

## Role of Women in Media Communication

At the United Nations Fourth World Conference on Women (FWCW), held at Beijing, China, in September 1996, one of the most striking features was the use of the information superhighway to speed the word about the Conference and the NGO Forum well beyond the boundaries of previous global conferences. In addition to the close to 40,000 participants, most of whom were women who had travelled to Beijing from all the corners of the globe, thousands of women and men joined the superhighway daily to follow the Conference and Forum using computers and telephone lines.

In the two years preceding the events, women and men from all regions, cultures and walks of life had reflected together on line, seeking consensus on fundamental issues related to gender and women's human rights. New computer networking technologies (CNTs) made this possible by broadening participation for diverse groups and enabling women in particular to participate and build new partnerships.

The UN's Division for the Advancement of Women (DAW), in its role as Secretariat for the Beijing Conference, worked to stimulate the use of computer technology for the Conference continues to see a role in facilitating its use in the follow-up to Beijing. In order to disseminate information on the Conference, DAW established a word Wide Web (WWW) site and, in collaboration with the United Nations Development Programme (UNDP), a local Internet server was set up at the official Conference venue.

The experience with electronic communicate networking at Beijing reflects the explosion in the field of communication technologies which have expanded global access to information at a remarkable rate. This revolution in information technology has created new opportunities as well as challenges. Just as advances in radio and television have seemed to transform our world into a "global village", CNTs have introduced a concept that changes the nature of space.

They have created a sphere, or cyberspace, where multiple and diverse opportunities for social interaction can evolve from the local to the planetary level. They have introduced an electronic "virtual community" where millions can come to share information and ideas as well as organize and mobilize for action on an unprecedented scale. This interaction can occur at a speed previously unheard of.

"The logic of networks is essentially a logic of spaces. Cyberspace itself is comprised of a vast conglomeration of data and information flow within which it is possible to define specific spaces where common interest groups gather to exchange information or co-ordinate activities". During the preparations for Beijing exchanges took place among women's organizations using several on-line instruments established by groups such as the Association for Progressive Communications (APC) and UNDP - electronic conferences or bulletin boards on specific topics, mailing lists, WWW pages, etc.

Organizations and individuals who used these spaces, including many who had indirect access through other organisations or by redisseminating information using traditional media, were better informed and able to prepare joint actions. This was an important factor in NGOs having a better-informed and -co-ordinated input at Beijing than at previous UN women's conferences. It has also been argued that by participating in these spaces, "many women and organizations are developing their experience and confidence to participate in other on-line circles and to publicly express their viewpoints.

Having access to an interactive space of communication provides women with opportunities to develop discourse with a prepositional focus, going beyond the rhetoric of denunciation and complaint.

Moreover, the new opportunities offered by electronic networks can be a training ground for women to develop the means of expression in the new media practices that will develop through this technology and in other media".

Electronic networking is fast becoming a fact of life, in both industrialized and developing countries. The electronic "superhighway" has made the communication of information more rapid and far-reaching than ever before in history. As the electronic highway evolves into a new mass medium, it is essential that women be fully involved in its development.

Experience in the past with other mass media has not always been positive for women. There is no guarantee that experience with the new CNTs will be any different. Negative stereotyping and discrimination against women as well as forms of sexual harassment on line are already evident. The Platform for Action (PfA) adopted at the FWCW called for women to take an active role in shaping the use of cyberspace to prevent similar patterns of abuse as seen in other mass media.

The Platform will be implemented at a time of rapid growth in the new information technologies. Since communications are at the heart of empowerment of people, women must ensure that the new technologies serve to empower them. Computer literacy is becoming an indispensable tool for organizing and mobilizing communities throughout the world, and women need to be directly involved in this new medium.

The Internet is a global network of computers linked by high-speed datalines and wireless systems. It was established in 1969 as a militarycommunications system.

It allows individuals to access information from manysources using a computer.

The use of the Internet more than doubled in sizein 1995 and has done so every year since 1988, becoming the fastest-growingcommunications medium ever. Measuring the real Internet population, its use disaggregated by sex,the size of the potential demand and the trends for growth is difficult, andresults are often contradictory.

The special nature of the medium and itsrapid development throw up new figures every day. Some sources have estimatedthat a new web site is launched on the Internet every four seconds. It is difficult to gauge reliably the size and demographic profile ofusers, because user-tracking software remains inadequate, and it is notpossible, for example, to distinguish new "hits" from repeat visits to a site.Nevertheless. it is estimated that the Internet links 50 million users in morethan 80 countries worldwide.

The WWW is the fastest-growing segment of the Internet, growing at rateof 3,000 per cent every year. It allows exchange of multimedia data (text,audio, video, graphics and animation) between users connected to the Internetusing hypertext links. In the United States, which has taken the lead in the market, datasuggest that there are between 16.4 million and 37 million people who have access to the Internet, spending an average of 5hours 28 minutes per week on line. Users in Europe are 5 to 8 million ormore.

In Japan, there are approximately 4 million users. In Latin America,electronic mail is rapidly replacing regular mail, as it is much moreefficient. In Africa, new Internet domains have been registered in the lastyear in Angola, Benin, Burkina Faso, Djibouti and Madagascar. In countriessuch as Kenya, Namibia and Senegal, the number of domains is rising rapidly.

In terms of market size, the global Internet market is expected to soarto $200 billion by the year 2000. The Internet Society expects 120 millionhosts to be connected to the Internet by the end of the decade, up from 9.5million in 1996. Investment bankers at Morgan Stanley project that thenumber of Web users will jump from 9 million in 1995 to more than 150 millionbyr 2000.

Markets for Internet-related products may be largely a function ofaccess. Many countries in the developing world do not have access tocomputers; some do not have reliable electricity or telephone service tosupport the CNTs, and in places where the capacity exists or is growing, thereis need for training, and for resources for time on line. Supporting technology transfer from industrialized to developingcountries, some assistance is being given by international organizations,bilateral donors and computer companies for acquisition of computers andtraining.

For example, since 1994 the United Nations Economic Commission forAfrica has increased the number of electronic domains -- mother computersunder which host computers are hooked into the Internet in Africa. The UNDPSustainable Development Networking Programme is heading an effort to bringconnectivity to developing countries in a participatory manner that wouldenable women's and other groups to have access to the Internet.

USAID, withthe Leland initiative, is another significant player -- focused on Africa. Use of the Internet is spreading rapidly because of the relatively lowcost of the basic infrastructure. However, the information revolution hascontinued to perpetuate many inequalities. The majority of people around theworld do not participate on an equal basis, either as participants or asproducers.

While the potential of the new medium has been recognized, it is clearthat until its use has spread to developing countries, and to all groups insociety, including women, it reinforces existing inequalities. The Taub Urban Research Center at New York University recently publisheda study based on data gathered by two consulting firms in the United States.Entitled "Leaders and Losers on the Internet", it addresses the impact of theInternet on urbanization. It notes that while many had predicted that globalcomputer networking could decentralize work and living patterns, to date theimpact of the Internet has been mainly to reinforce the economic andintellectual leadership of a handful of urban centres and nearby suburbs.

While the new medium includes the potential for democratizinginformation and communications as a result of its interactive andparticipatory nature, evidence suggests that fewer women than men use the newtechnologies and that the computer environment is often hostile or denigratingto women and includes forms of sexual harassment. Women, nevertheless, area fast-growing segment of the Internet's user population.

Most of thefemale users seem to be located in North America, especially in the UnitedStates. Even in the United States, the estimate of female Internet usersvaries from 29 per cent to 36 per cent. Surveys have shown that men are much more likely than women to use theWWW.

However, women are slightly more likely than men to use Internet E-mailand to participate in Internet mailing lists, underscoring a strongpredisposition among women toward Internet communications features.

Womenare also more likely than men to use the Internet exclusively from work oracademic locations, while men are more likely to use it from multiplelocations, including after-hours use from home. Internet Navigation needs to be more intuitive. With men, the computer tends to be perceived as a gadget... . Women see the computer more as an efficiency vehicle.

The contribution of women to Internet tools such as the UseNetnewsgroups is "typically not very high, but the actual numbers are subject todebate. In the unmoderated feminist newgroups, approximately 80 per cent ofthe messages are posted by men. In the moderated feminist groups, there isusually about a 50/50 balance between women and men."

Different networksattract different audiences. SeniorNet, a consumer-oriented on-line-serviceavailable on America On-line that caters to the 'mature market', reports thattheir audience mix is 51 per cent female and 49 per cent male. For otherservices such as CompuServe, Genie and Prodigy "between 60-90 per cent of thecustomers are male."

## Role of Women in information superhighway

The Women's Networking Support Program of APC has recently conducted a survey on women's experiences with electronic networking. Early results are from 30 countries in Africa, Asia and the Pacific, Eastern Europe, Western Europe, Latin America, Western Asia and North

America. Initial findings indicated that women are increasingly active in using electronic communications, and that many tools such as E-mail have become a routine part of their day-to-day communications activity.

Increasingly, women are experimenting with on-line conferences, mailing lists and web sites. At the same time, the survey showed that women continue to face barriers in using the information superhighway, such as lack of training and the high cost of equipment and, in some places, of getting connected. Networking has been recognized by female scholars as a tool for women's empowerment, and women have taken to the Net to create a "cyberspace of their own."

In many places, women writers, editors, news directors and lobbyists, are not only surfing the Net, but have become active in establishing numerous sites of special interest to women on the WWW. Women's sites cover subjects such as gender and sexuality, feminism, women's health, women in computer science, engineering, women's studies, women in academia and women in industry.

Research carried out for the UN Division for the Advancement of Women found that women were initially less present on the electronic networks than men, and that not surprisingly, certain circles have developed on the Internet that are characterized by a male-dominated and patriarchal on-line culture which discriminates against women or treats them negatively.

But women face two particular challenges in their use of computer networks. The first is to master access tools so they can make the best use of CNTs. The second is to use the new Internet publishing tools to develop their own publishing and media activities on the networks as paradigms of gender-sensitive media products.

The women's movement has long been critical of mass media, charging that they are deeply implicated in reinforcing patterns of discrimination against women in society. An analysis of sex roles and stereotypes indicates that few reports deal with issues of special concern to women or reflect a gender perspective. In relation to CNTs, this is a crucial moment. The rules of the game are still in formulation.

Women, therefore, need to discuss the need for gender- sensitive information; participate in decision-making on network development and evolve alternative and gender-sensitive practices. Women need to decide whether they will create their own closed spaces on the Internet or assert their presence in mixed spaces. And once again, the answer is, surely, both. Without this kind of action, we can expect that the new medium will increasingly be yet another means to perpetuate negative stereotypes, or another male enclave where women are discriminated against and marginalized.

Women have increasingly created alternative communications outside the mainstream media to counteract discrimination and stereotyping. Independent alternative media controlled by women include print media, video, film, radio broadcasting and, increasingly, the CNTs. Women have created and used alternative communication channels to support their efforts, defend their rights, diffuse their own forms of representation and question dominant models of mainstream culture.

With the advent of the CNTs, women are also finding ways to use them to support their advocacy efforts. For example, women's groups in Mexico have found that electronic networking has facilitated their work in fighting NAFTA. Groups are also appearing that help women gain access and training.

For example, WON, the Women's Online Network, is an on-line advocacy and action group which is sponsored by various women's groups. Women are taking new steps and increasingly moving in new directions by networking electronically ... these days it is not unusual to see women's networks and organizations making the most of new information and communication tools to get their message out and make their voices heard."

The new media are a logical extension of alternative forms of media previously used by women. They have characteristics similar to those of the alternative media, and suited to the needs of women's networks because of their decentralized and horizontal nature. The essential difference from the mainstream media is their relation to space.

The challenge is to maintain the Internet as an open communication system with democratic access to information and not as a centrally controlled medium. For women's organizations, this may mean establishing and defining their own spaces or influencing the character of on-line culture in favour of gender balance and non-discrimination. Recognizing the speed and importance of technological changes in electronic communications, the PfA adopted by consensus in Beijing called on organizations at all levels to increase the participation and access of women to expression and decision-making in and through the media and new technologies as a means of strengthening women's participation in democratic processes.

The PfA identified the need for access, training and network development for women. Women should be empowered by enhancing their skills, knowledge and access to the information technology. This will strengthen their ability to combat negative portrayals of women internationally and to challenge instances of abuse of power of an increasingly important industry... Women therefore need to be involved in decision-making regarding the development of the new technologies in order to participate fully in their growth and impact.

The Platform called on international organizations, Governments, media systems, NGOs and media professional organizations to increase the participation and access of women to expression and decision-making in and through the media and new technologies of communication. Concerned about the image of women projected in the media, participants at the FWCW agreed that "print and electronic media in most countries do not provide a balanced picture of women's diverse lives and contributions to society in a changing world."

The PfA called for a "balanced portrayal of women and girls in their multiple roles" and encouraged the "use of non-stereotyped, balanced and diverse images of women in the media". The PfA also requested the mass media and advertising organizations "to develop, consistent with freedom of expression, professional guidelines and codes of conduct and other forms of self-regulation to promote the presentation of non-stereotyped images of women" and "that address violent, degrading or pornographic materials concerning women ... ".

At its fortieth session, in March 1996, the United Nations Commission on the Status of Women (CSW), the main intergovernmental body focusing on women, and delegates, experts and NGOs examined the measures proposed in the PfA and agreed that advances in information technology had opened up boundaries.

It was agreed that the role of women in global communication networks needed to be strengthened, and that barriers to information technology and to women's involvement at every level of its development should be reduced. Notably, several organizations and bodies held meetings in this field in preparation for the Beijing Conference. One important gathering to assess strategies and plans for using electronic networking was held in Bangkok from 12 to 17 February 1994.

The "Women Empowering Communication" conference was sponsored by the World Association for Christian Communication (WACC) in association with ISIS International and the International Women's Tribune Centre (IWTC). More than 400 women from over 80 countries participated. As a result of the meeting, the Bangkok Declaration was adopted, which emphasized strengthening women's communication networks. UNESCO convened an international symposium on "Women and the Media: access to expression and decision-making" in Toronto, Canada, from 28 February to 3 March 1995.

A Platform for Action was adopted which stressed the need for greater involvement of women in both the technical and decision-making areas of communication and media. The symposium was attended by over 170 media professionals from more than 70 countries, and its results served as an important input to the negotiations on women and the media at Beijing.

Following the Conference, UNESCO and the Society for International Development are studying the culture of the Internet and its potential as an effective tool for women. The project, "Women and Cyberculture", analyses the impact of globalized communications from a gender perspective. Sexual harassment is also identified in Chapter J of the PfA as one of the acts of gender-based violence encompassed under the critical area "Violence against women".

On the Internet, harassment presents an important issue for women. It has occurred in both public forums and private E-mail. It takes different forms and can be subtle, such as personal questions directed to a woman, or blatant, such as sexual propositions to women via E-mail. The Internet neutralizes social status indicators such as appearance, voice, organizational hierarchy and often sex.

# 3

# Internet Media

What generally stand in the way of people's understanding of New Media are the very terms media and medium. As commonly used, those terms are misnomers that block understanding. Very few people understand the New Media simply because what most people think are media are actually vehicles within a medium. Magazines aren't media nor is a magazine a medium.

Television isn't a medium nor is radio nor are television stations media. A personal computer connected to the Internet isn't a medium and the many computers that comprise the Internet aren't media. Neither is the World Wide Web a medium nor is e-mail a medium nor is the Internet itself a medium.

Newspapers, magazines, television, radio, telephones, billboards, personal computers, the Internet, the World Wide Web, and e-mail all are vehicles for conveying information within a medium or media. They aren't the media or a medium in which they operate.

To understand the difference between a communications vehicle and a communications medium, you merely need to understand how the terms medium, media, and vehicles are correctly used when discussing transportation. Indeed, you will then also understand that only three communications media exist, what those three are, and how to use them.

Here is the analogy between communications media and transportation media. Take a minute to read it. Only three transportation media exist. Land was the aboriginal transportation medium; it was the first transportation medium. Humans have has walked on it since time immemorial. Water is the second transportation medium. Its use as a transportation medium is almost as old as humanity's use of land, dating from whenever the first human attempted to ride a floating log or to swim across a stream, river, or lake.

The vehicles that human technology created have merely extended our speed and carrying capacities in those media. For examples, water vehicles have almost global reach but not to landlocked cities. Land vehicles can deliver door-to-door, a capability that water vehicle can't provide. But many water vehicles have much greater carrying capacities than do land vehicles.

Throughout most of human history, people were limited to those two transportation media and those media's mutual advantages and disadvantages. But in 1783 two French brothers named Montgolfier used their era's technology to vehicle that transported them into an entirely new medium. A hundred years later, Otto Lilenthal fabricated the technology of airfoils and began gliding over the German countryside, ponds, and lakes.

And 20 years after that, two American brothers named Wright determined how to marry an engine to a glider. Utilizing technology, these pioneers opened a third transportation medium that until then had been little more than a dream — the Sky. Other vehicles developed for this new transportation medium are balloons, parachutes, gliders, airplanes, helicopters, and lately, spacecraft.

These are vehicles that can transport people anywhere on Earth. Though the transportation media of land and water have mutually exclusive reaches, this new transportation medium of the sky encompasses the reaches of both land and water, and generally without the complementary advantages and disadvantages of those two prior media. But note that this new transportation medium of the sky is entirely dependent upon technology, unlike the two prior media.

The sky isn't a natural medium for humans; people can walk and swim but we cannot fly. Just as only three transportation media exist, only three communications media exist. As with transportation media, two of those communication media are ancient and arose independent of technology. This aboriginal medium arose in basic animal communications, predating both humans and technology.

Human technology later extended its speed and reach. Interpersonal conversation is the basic form of this medium. The vehicles that human technology later built for it include the postal letter, telephone call, and electronic mail. Just as the transportation media of land or water have some unique characteristics, so does the this Interpersonal Medium of communications. It notably has two hallmarks:

— Each participant has equal and reciprocal control of the content conveyed.

— And the content can be individualized to each participant's unique needs and interests.

However, those hallmark advantages come with equal disadvantages: The equal control and also the individualization of content degrade into cacophony as the number of participants increases beyond two (for example, try simultaneously holding different conversations with more than one person).

For those reasons, this Interpersonal Medium characteristically is used for communications between only two people. And why many academics who study communications media term it the 'one-to-one' medium.

Most people mistake the Mass Medium as a product of technology and don't realize how old it really is. Like the Interpersonal Medium, the Mass Medium predates technology. It originated with the utterances and speeches of tribal leaders, kings, and priests.

Technology has merely extended its speed and its reach to global dimensions. Some vehicles in the Mass Medium are edicts, oratory, sermons, scriptures, plays, books, newspapers, billboards, magazines, cinema, radio, television, bulletin boards, and webcasting. Communications in the Mass Medium generally go from a one person (for examples, a leader, a king, a priest, a publisher, or a broadcaster) to many people (the audience, readership, listenership, viewership).

This also is why many academics who study communications media term it the 'one-to-many' medium. The hallmark characteristics of the Mass Medium are:

— That the same content goes to all recipients.

— And that the one who sends it has absolute control over that content.

The corresponding disadvantages of the Mass Medium are:

— That its content cannot be individualized to each recipient's unique needs and interests and that the recipients have no real control over that content.

— Like the Interpersonal Medium, the Mass Medium isn't necessarily dependent upon technology. For example, an actor or speaker can perform without any technology.

Just as the transportation media of land and water have mutually exclusive characteristics, so do the Interpersonal Medium and the Mass Medium for communications:

— The Interpersonal Medium can deliver an individualized message but only to one person at a time.

— The Mass Medium can simultaneously deliver messages to an infinite number of people but its messages cannot be individualized for each recipient.

— The Interpersonal Medium allows each participant equal control over the content.

— The Mass Medium allows control over the content by only one person.

Those mutually exclusive characteristics of the Interpersonal and Mass media have been important because anyone who wants to individually communicate a unique message to each recipient has had to use the vehicles of Interpersonal Medium. And anyone who wants at once to communicate message to a mass of people has had to use the vehicles of the Mass Medium.

Just like using the sky as a transportation medium, for most of human history the possibility of any third communications medium existing had been inconceivable. Anyone needing to communicate had to choose between the mutually incompatible characteristics of the Interpersonal and the Mass media.

But, Just like how several technologies converged nearly a century ago to make the sky a transportation medium, the evolution of several ostensibly unrelated technologies converged during the past century to create a third and entirely new communications medium. Among those convergent technologies were:

— The invention of digital communications during the late 1940s;

— The invention of the Transport Control/Internet Protocol ((TCP/IP) in the late 1960s;

— ARPANET's creation of the Internet during the early 1970s;

— The invention of the personal computer in the late 1970s.

And to lesser degrees of the importance:

— The invention of the HyperText Transport Protocol (HTTP) in the late 1980s;

— The opening of the Internet to the public in 1992;

— The invention of the Mosaic browser software in that same year.

— These and other technological innovations converged to create a new communications medium that has characteristics inconceivable even a decade ago.

The hallmark characteristics of this New Medium are:

— That individualized messages can simultaneously be delivered to an infinite number of people.

— And that each of the people involved shares reciprocal control over that content.

— In other words, the New Medium has the advantages of both the Interpersonal and the Mass media, but without their complementary disadvantages.

No longer must anyone who wants to individually communicate a unique message to each recipient have to be restricted to communicating with only one person at a time. No longer must anyone who wants at once to communicate message to a mass of people be unable to individualized totally the content of that message for each recipient.

The New Medium for communications, like the transportation medium of the sky, is entirely dependent upon technology, unlike the two preceding communications media. Like humans flying with technology, this form of communications can't be done with technology.

Because the New Medium simultaneously encompasses both the characteristics and the reach of the two previous communication media and therefore can easily perform each of those media's individual tasks, many people mistake the New Medium as merely an electronic extension of the Interpersonal or Mass media.

Most people mistake it as a paperless or antenna-less form of the Mass Medium (a mistake somewhat like seeing aviation only from the perspective of the ground.) Moreover, many marketing consultants often mistakenly refer to it as a 'one-to-one' medium.

But the academic and the consultants who truly understand this New Medium and its possibilities to simultaneously deliver an infinite number of individualized messages while providing equal control over that content refer to the New Medium as the 'many-to-many' medium — to distinguish it from the 'one-to-one' (Interpersonal) or 'one-to-many' (Mass) media.

Mistakes, misnomers, and misperceptions of the New Medium are easy to make because the vehicles of this New Medium are only starting to appear, as are the true capabilities of this New Medium. For instance, the millions of computers interconnected through the Internet can acquire, sort, package, and transmit information in as many ways as there are individual people. They can establish those communications simultaneously. And they allow each participant (senders and receivers) to share equal simultaneous control.

This can result in unprecedented forms of communications. Imagine that when a person visits a newspaper Web site, he sees not just the bulletins and major stories that he wouldn't have known to request information about but sees the rest of that edition customized to his own unique needs and interests. Rather than every reader seeing the same edition, each reader sees an edition that has simultaneously been individualized to his interest and generalized to his needs.

Realize that these New Medium forms of content inherently are forms of mass customization, something impossible with either the Interpersonal Medium or the Mass Medium. The existence of this New Medium will catalyze, economize, and popularize entirely new vehicles for production and distribution, just as the invention of the medium of air did for transportation.

And it will create entirely new concepts in and forms of content. The personalized web site is one (personalized actually is another misnomer; individualized is a more accurate term). Some computer games, such as Myst, are New Medium vehicles. Napster is a New Medium vehicle.

Other New Medium vehicles are only now being developed as entrepreneurs and companies realize this medium's possibilities. The New Medium itself is merely a manifestation of a larger, revolutionary historical change underway that transcends just issues of communications.

Analysts and pundits talk about this larger change as an Informational Revolution that is superceding the world of the Industrial Revolution in much in the same way that the Industrial Revolution itself superceded the Agrarian Revolution. But the terms Informational, Industrial, and Agrarian merely refer to characteristic products of these phases in the evolution of human society. Not to the natures of these revolutions themselves.

During the Agrarian world, which began about 5,000 to 10,000 years ago, a person who needed clothing had to make his clothing himself. Or another person made his clothing individually for him. Only one piece of clothing would be made at a time and each piece of clothing would be individualized to his own individual size and needs.

Then some 200 years ago, mechanical technology evolved to the point where factories could created, and the Industrial Revolution began. In the Industrial world, millions of pieces of clothing could be produced, but none could be individualized to the exact measurements of its ultimate consumer. How these complementary advantages and disadvantages of products from the Agrarian and Industrial ages are similar to the complementary advantages and disadvantages of the Interpersonal Medium and the Mass Medium.

This is because most of what we nowadays perceive to be the Interpersonal Medium dates from the Agrarian Revolution and most of what we nowadays perceive to be the Mass Medium dates from the Industrial Revolution. Now, new advancements have created technologies that unite the advantages of both Agrarian individualized production and Industrial mass production, with none of the complementary disadvantages.

For example, companies using these new technologies,such as Levis Strauss & Co., have begun to mass-produce jeans that are individualized to each users exact specifications. This is similar to how the New Medium can send instantly individualized messages to mass of recipients. Both the New Medium and Levis Strauss & Co.'s abilities to mass produce of individualized jeans are manifestations of the Informational Revolution.

The Informational Revolution's effects upon society are being compared to those from the invention and promulgation of printing presses. However, the actual significance of the Informational Revolution is greater: The invention of the printing press was merely a technological amplification of the Mass Medium.

By contrast, this New Medium indeed is an entirely new medium; a quantum leap beyond mere innovations such as the printing press. Returning to our analogy between transportation and communications media, the development of the air as transportation medium didn't entirely replace land or sea transportation.

Neither will the development of this new communication medium entirely replace the Interpersonal or the Mass media. However, it will certainly and markedly reduce and limit those previous media, much as the invention of aviation did to land and sea transportation. So, if you don't now understand what the New Medium is and how it differs from traditional media, please let us know.

## Fundamentals Traits of the New Medium

The practical value of these Traits is as indicators of any New Medium venture's prospects for success. Four Fundamental traits differentiate the New Medium from previous media. Other apparent traits of the New Medium can be reduced to these four common denominators. Although each of these four traits is distinct, none alone created the New Medium.

These traits instead have a stratal relationship (i.e., the second trait builds upon the first trait, the third trait upon the first two traits, etc.). Their resultant cascading interactions fomented the Informational Revolution and continue to propel an accelerating evolution in communication media. Any competently managed endeavor that utilizes all four traits will succeed. Any competently managed endeavor that utilizes three might succeed. But any competently managed endeavor that utilizes only one or two of these traits will likely to fail.

The Four Fundamental Ttraits of the New Medium are:

— As Nicholas Negroponte succinctly put it, 'Bits, Not Atoms'

— Digital Addressability.

— A Quantum Shift in Control Towards Consumers.

— Open, Autonomous Systems Triumph over Closed, Proprietary Systems.

Nicholas Negroponte means that information and non-consumable services, now and into the future, will increasingly be delivered in the form of electronic bits and not as physical atoms of material and packaging. Words, images, sounds, software, data, plus as many non-consumable services as economically practicable, will be distributed electronically, rather than in the traditional forms of paper, disks, boxes, or other physical materials.

The propagation of information and similar services no longer has to contend with the costs and delays of physical delivery. Digital Deliverance of information and services is weightless and moves at nearly the speed of light. Delivery thus is nearly instantaneous worldwide.

The concepts of an address and of digital transmission of information are each old. Addresses have existed since perhaps the day when one caveman gave directions to another caveman to find the cave of a third. The contemporary version of addresses certainly dates from the invention of postal services during the 1700s.

Digital Transmission of information is nearly 50 years old, originally used by the vacuum tube computers immediately after the Second World War. For most of time since, however, digital transmission of information merely involved communications within a single computer and its peripherals. What is new and remarkable is the combination of addressability and digital transmission.

This is a very recent combination with remarkable capabilities. The combination allows information and various services to be delivered instantaneously, discreetly, and discretely to virtually everyone. The fundamental trait of Digital Addressability leads to two corollaries:

— Individualization (the colloquial misnomer is Personalization).

— A triumph of individualized products & services triumph over non-individualized products & services

Each evolution in media shifts control farther out of the hands of the persons who operate the media and more into the hands of the people who use it. Control always shifts somewhat more from the one to the many. That each evolution in media technology always shifts control farther away from the one and more towards the many is a historical fact, visible over the millennia.

Such shift are generally quite rapid, shifting farther and faster than might have been expected. Indeed, these evolutions are characterized by quantum ('a sudden or sufficient amount.') shifts in control . Nowadays, the recent proliferation of digital technologies into the hands of consumers has shifted control of the media farther and more suddenly into their hands than at any time in history.

Quantum shifts in control over media occurred with the developments of cuneiform, papyrus (paper), the printing press, and the telephone. Historically, early media were under the singular controls of a leader of a tribe, church, or state, who operated by edicts, proclamations, sermons, town criers, or sanctioned theater. An example of a quantum shift occured immediately after Johannes Gutenberg's invention of the moveable-type printing press.

Control over media at that time had been in the singular hands of the aristocracy and the church, due to the huge labor and expense required to scribe each book or broadside by hand. But Gutenberg's invention unfettered that control, shifting it further out of the hands of the aristocracy and church and more into the hands of the many (that is, those many who could afford a printing press).

Within 30 years of his invention, over three million printing presses were operating in Europe. These quantum shifts provide consumers with more choices of media vehicles, and more diverse information and opinion. In fact, a hallmark of these quantum shifts is that it occurs without causation by a government, church, or corporation — constituencies that don't want to lose further control over media.

In the half-millennium since Gutenberg, control over media control hadn't significantly shifted again until fairly recently, when development of technology began to accelerate. Although the Industrial Era inventions of the telegraph by Samuel F.B. Morse and of the wireless transmitter by Guglielmo Marconi globalized the reach and speed of communications, each of those did not significantly cause a shift in control of media.

However, Alexander Graham Bell's invention of telephony did. It gave the masses themselves the capabilities to convey information immediately anywhere, without intervening controls. It greatly increased the diversity of opinion and information worldwide. Like foreshadowing shakes that precurse a major shift, several analog media technologies connected to telephones did encourage enough of a shift in control to actually help rattle governments during the last half of the 20th Century.

For examples, zamisdat underground publications, produced on typewriters or xerography, roiled Eastern European dictatorships in the 1960s and 1970s. Similar underground publications, distributed via xerographic facsimile machines communicating by telephony, distressed the Chinese mainland government in the late 1980s. It is therefore perhaps ironic that the Internet — a originally designed as a survivable, unrestrictable communications network for a government — has nowadays created a quantum shift in control more towards the hands of the many and not the one.

The recent proliferation of digital technologies in the hands of consumers, combined with public access to the Internet beginning in 1992, has shifted control of the media farther and more suddenly into their hands than at any time in history. Indeed, control may have shifted onto, or even over, its traditional fulcrum point, ending centuries of relatively relatively one-sided control by publishers of media.

Like democracy overthrowing aristocracy, this trait is characteristic of truly revolutionary change. Industrial Era technological and business theory stated that systems would be most successful if proprietarily self-contained. For examples, each operator of early railroads would use track of different width to prevent competitors rolling along them.

Later, distributors of products were taught to monopolize and limit the number of channels of distribution. Until the 1990s, communications protocols would be invented that intentionally weren't interoperable with any other communication protocols. A manufacturer would invent something that could be connected only to other products manufactured by that company. Software couldn't be plugged into other software.

That era ended about 1992, around the time that the communication network known as the Internet, which until then had been restricted to use by the U.S. government and its contractors, was opened to the public and to commerce. Arising from the previous four Fundamental Traits of the New Medium, the Internet has a novel characteristic: It is an open and autonomous system.

No one governs or owns it. Its communications protocols are public and nonproprietary. Ad those protocols are open and interoperable. According to Industrial Era theory, the Internet's widespread adoption by the public and commerce stood little chance against well funded and well marketed proprietary and closed online systems such as IBM and Sears's Prodigy, H&R Block's CompuServe, America Online, General Electric's GEnie, and News Corporation (Rupert Murdoch)'s Delphi for the consume realm and MCI, Sprint, AT&T, NTT, Deutsche Telekom, Cable & Wireless, and other telecommunications firms for the business realm.

Yet, the Internet spontaneously triumphed over those proprietary and closed systems. One reason was that the Internet's open nature allowed consumers to have far more access to the information they need to live their lives than was provided by the closed systems. Another reason was that the Internet's open architecture and protocols allowed thousands of software and hardware vendors to manufacture products that utilized it; compared to the expense and travail of having to license the architecture and protocols of any of the proprietary systems.

By 2002, more than 500 million consumers worldwide were utilizing the Internet. Two relatively recent examples of this Trait are in the personal computer field and the music industry:

IBM's belated attempts to proprietize PC architecture through OS/2, which at the time might have been a technologically superior operating system, was vanquished by the more open, if no less proprietary, Microsoft Windows 3.1. Likewise, the Macintosh Apple line hobbled itself during the late 1980s by initially keeping its system proprietary and closed.

The accessibility and lower costs of open technological systems means these systems become adopted more swiftly and more often than closed or proprietary systems will be. Swift adoption means open systems quickly beget add-ons, plug-ins, and other enhancements that secure an open system as the foundation for a new standard.

Napster was perhaps the premiere example of open and autonomous systems triumphing over close and proprietary ones. Napster's rise stunned the music industry at the turn of the century. Although the music industry beat Napster through legalistic means, that industry probably won't be as successsful fighting off Napster's successors (such as Morpheus) that now have the legalistic advantange of being so open and automous that they have no entity for the music industry to sue.

## Revolutionary Changes in Learning

Nevertheless, many businesses have begun to see the practical advantages of understanding this trait. Crucial operations tend to run more efficiently, profilically, and practically when run by interdependent, interdisciplinary teams in the field, rather than run exclusively or micro-managed by hierarchical bureaucracies, command centers, or boardrooms.

The military also has been adopting such new hierarchal operations. Businesses also have taken notice that the accessibility and lower costs of open systems means that such systems become adopted more swiftly and more often than can any closed or proprietary system. Swift adoption means open systems quickly beget add-ons, plug-ins, and other enhancements that secure an open system as the foundation for a new standard.

Business schools for decades had taught that any company's products and services should be made proprietary, but many progressive business school are now teaching that such systems should be opened and autonomous. Open, autonomous systems function more effectively, prolifically, and practically than closed, hierarchical systems. This Trait actually is only a manifestation of a larger, revolutionary historical change underway that transcends issues of communications.

It is part of the Information Revolution that is superceding the world of the Industrial Revolution in much in the same way that the Industrial Revolution itself superceded the Agrarian Revolution. Moreover, science, politics, and business have only in the past few decades begun to understand how open, autonomous system are actually natural.

Only several decades ago did mainstream science begin to understand that the natural environment itself is an open and autonomous system; that it is globally interdependent and not bounded by any geopolitical or cultural borders. Only 25 years ago did business and finance begin to realize that, with technological advances, currency and equity trading was becoming an open and autonomous system, no longer bounded by any geopolitical or cultural borders, indeed fully capable of bypassing any centralized or hierarchical geopolitical controls.

Only about ten years ago did politicians on the world's largest continents ultimately realize that centralized political planning and centralized economic planning and implementation of such through closed and hierarchical systems naturally fail and that open and autonomous systems triumph.

The 20th Century's long experimentions with fascism and communism failed, superced by open and autonomous democracratic systems. Likewise, science has only recently begun realizing that the most complex processes known — such the operations of the brain or of weather — naturally function as huge open and autonomous systems.

Closed, hierarchical systems are human fabrications, not natural creations. We are only now beginning to recognizing that all things consummate or divine work as open, autonomous, and interdependent systems. This Fundamental Trait of the New Medium has some direct corollaries. Any open and autonomous system will grow to vanquish any single or aggregate closed or hierarchical system of equal function.

Horizontally extensible open and autonomous systems tend to vanquish those that are only vertically extensible. Any corporation or media company that plans a New Medium endeavor should not limit the abilities of consumers' to travel or function outside that endeavor and not limit them solely to proprietary content.

## Communication Crisis in Internet Media

With the Internet a new media has appeared, which on the one hand has increased the risk associated with information: free accessibility, interactivity, globality, and connectivity of personal, economical, political and media communication have all led to a loss of journalistic control over the information market.

On the other hand Internet-based communication has increased opportunities to secure information in a manner that has not been available up to now. In terms of crisis communication this leads to the question: does the Internet increase or decrease the risk of a communication breakdown? It has been demonstrated that trust is one of the features in complex modern societies which compensates for risk.

If there is one event which gave us the proof and sharpened our awareness, that we live in a global risk society, it was the September 11th 2001 attack on the cities of New York and Washington, when four planes were hijacked, two of them slammed into the towers of the World Trade Center, one into the Pentagon and the last crashed in a field near Pittsburgh.

The hidden risks of globalisation as poverty, unemployment, environmental damage and cultural conflicts became apparent and evident at a glance. The pictures of the burning towers of the World Trade Center made it clear that globalisation is not a one-way street starting in the industrialized countries and ending in the developing countries. Rather globalisation is a kind of network effect for which communication plays an important role.

Even the symbolism of the attacks, which hit the military and the economical centres of American culture, demonstrate a kind of communicative impact. How crisis communication on a global level via the Internet works could also be observed very clearly in the coverage and the worldwide communication about the September 11th events.

From a special point of view, the communication of these events, and the subsequent Anthrax attacks, is a paradigm in crisis communication—and especially in crisis communication where the Internet plays a crucial role. I will therefore use this case to show some aspects of the interrelationship between crisis communication and the Internet. Very soon after the September events headlines, like the following, appeared:

— Media critics see Web role emerge
— Internet matures as news source
— Internet performs global role, supplementing TV
— From Niche Site to news portal
— Anthrax fears send visitors to Web

In an editorial of the leading Internet survey service NUA, it was stated on 17 September:

> "In the past week, the Internet was more than it has ever been before. Not only were those of us at a distance able to read first-hand, up-to-date reports of what was happening, but those survivors who were caught up in the chaos were able to email and send instant messages to family, friends, and colleagues to reassure them. When the phone system collapsed, the Internet came through".

Sixty-four percent of Americans used the Internet to find information on the attacks. They went online to find more detailed information, to find information they could not get elsewhere, to find more up-to-date information, and to find out what was happening while they were at work. The Internet was also an important secondary source of information, whereas television remains the most used primary information source.

More than 17 million users visited the CNN Web site. The number of German online surfers who used American Web sites doubled between the 10-16 September. Traffic to the Web site for the Centers for Disease Control and Prevention surged by more than 118 percent during the week of 7 October, according to Nielsen/NetRatings, a Web audience measurement company. The Web site drew about a half million visitors, and more than 250,000 looked up pages containing information on the symptoms, diagnosis and treatment of anthrax.

As a result of September 11th, there were not only increases in overall Internet traffic but the traffic became more international and more intercultural. And that is maybe the most interesting aspect of the whole issue. Normally, empirical research on linking patterns on the Internet for the year 2000 indicate that "national cultures continue to exert a substantial influence on how transnational connections are made".

So normally 90 percent of links on U.S. Web sites are directed to other U.S. sites and in European countries about between 60 and 70 percent of the links refer to Web site locally or nationally. If European Web sites point to sites across national borders, 70 percent of the links from Europe are directed to U.S. Web sites.

Information from Hitwise, which tracks traffic to the most popular news sites, demonstrated that traffic to sites such as the Islamic Gateway, Dawn.com (national newspaper of Pakistan), ExpressIndia.com, HindustanTimes.com, and Haaretz.co.il (Israeli newspaper) grew noticeably in the aftermath of the September 11th attacks. The biggest increase in traffic was that of Afghanistan Online, which jumped more than 11,000 places in the Hitwise rankings. Traffic to Al Jazeera.net, the site of the independent Middle East television station, also soared.

The online edition of Germany's most influential news magazin Der Spiegel covered a story, in which they portrayed some of the online news sites from Islamic countries, to support German online user in searching foreign news. The regional newspaper in Minneapolis, the Pioneer Press presented its readers the same service of portraying some of the Arabic and Islamic Web sites.

What became rather clear from this facts: research on crisis communication of today cannot ignore that the Internet has become an important source and mode of communication in times of crisis, especially, when they are of global character. Does the growing importance of the Internet contribute to an improvement in international crisis communication and crisis journalism or is it just another channel for distributing the same old stuff in the same old pattern of news coverage, dominated by exactly the sources that should be objects of the coverage?

To get a better grasp of crisis communication on the Internet we will use some terms or concepts introduced by Anthony Giddens in his analysis of the consequences of modernity: the terms of risk and trust. Concerning the concept of risk he relied heavily on the German sociologist Ulrich Beck, who declared that risk is the main feature of modern societies.

But risk is not an objective quality, risk is a construction, which means that we have to deal with the perception of risk rather than an objective feature of the world. If a construction is public and is part of a common knowledge, this could be analysed as a result of public communication: we know what others know only if we take part a the same communicational exchange. So risk perception could turn into a common view of the world, if this knowledge is communicated.

In term of knowledge we can define crisis as a situation of uncertainty: we don't know enough to understand what happens and we are lacking knowledge about a way out or a loophole. That means we are always acting under the risk of making a wrong decision. The more complex a situation is, the higher that risk. As Beck demonstrated risk is a characteristic feature of modern society, as complexity on one side makes it difficult to find adequate solutions, and in turn, decisions are irreversible.

Risk is, in words of constructivism, a "construct of the observer". Risk and trust are not objective categories but subjective categories. And they are subjective in a deep sense: neither you can command a person to trust in you or someone or something nor can you command a person not to feel uncertain or risky. Risk and trust are built up in communication. Media communication has a double connection with risk. First, media should transfer knowledge that helps us to minimize uncertainty. Second, media itself has become a risk, a risk of information.

One can add that they come from media coverage and information outlets as much as a lack of them. We need another term to get a better understanding of the role of the Internet in crisis communication, the term of disembedding, which was introduced by Giddens. Disembedding means "the lifting out of social relations from local contexts of interaction and their restructuring across indefinite span of times". From this point of view all media communication is disembedded, as it leaves behind the direct face-to-face-communication.

But the Internet is the most disembedded media as it is the most removed from face-to-face-communication. In Internet communication we first do not have the limitations of space: there are no borders for circulation and there is unlimited memory space for content. This dimension of disembedding constitutes the globalisation of the medium. Second, we have no time limitations, which means messages can be posted at any time, communicators do not have to wait for datelines of publishing.

Coverage can happen in real-time, without any delay for production and distribution, and as one should add without any quality control. Third, we have no limitations on the roles of communicators and participants: whoever has the technical capacities to receive messages with a computer is also able to send them.

He can do that without restrictions on his or her role, be it as a commentator, a reporter, a businessman, citizen, or a politician. Finally, on the Internet there are no limitations of content. "All the news that fit to print" is no longer a limitation on Internet content. Content can take many forms on the Internet, videotaped, audiotaped or visualized.

"News" can take many forms from text to games to letters. This high degree of disembeddedness makes Internet communication highly risky, because disembedding always means loss of control: control over sources and their reliability, control over selection, control over verification. We have to cope with the problem of informational risk and of communication collapse.

Trust is normally a means to compensate for our lack of knowledge in handling complex systems. Trust reduces uncertainty. It does not make up for lack of knowledge, but it allows us to believe and act as if we were in a state of full and certain knowledge. Hence the Internet plays a double-edged role in crisis communication.

On the one hand, it increases the risk of information thanks to the loss of traditional journalistic controls over the information market. We no longer have an expert system to which we can assign management of information quality. On the other hand, the Internet extends the possibilities of getting information in a manner that has not been available up to now.

It strengthens the informational self-determination of the audience and make them more independent of traditional media. In the media, it turned out very clearly that the Internet from one perspective improved crisis communication while on the other side the Internet made it more difficult, more risky. Generally, the dark side of the Internet in crisis communications is mirrored in limited access to certain kinds of information; Rumours and hoaxes; False information; and, Bias.

These factors all affect informational uncertainty. Examples abound from the events of September 11th. In a leading article, with the headline "Information please", the New York Times stated:

> "Fear has been fueled by the fitful and sometimes contradictory flow of information from the government and by the sometimes sloppy and slow response on the ground. (...) The frequent lack of specificity in the government's warnings and information has also heightened public fear. On Thursday, the Justice Department warned of imminent terrorist attacks, as soon as the weekend, but said it had no information about where the new threats might come. They did not link those warnings to anthrax."

The following rumors show typical aspects of Internet communication: they were spread with high speed and globally; they induced notice by all types of media; and, they were countered by online information:

— a Nostradamus prophecy anticipated the attack on the World Trade Center;

— a coded message predicting the attack was found in Microsoft's "Wingdings" graphics font designed long before the recent events;

— 4,000 Jews were warned against going to the World Trade Center on the day of the attack;

— photos of the burning buildings reveal the face of Satan in clouds of smoke;

— another wave of terrorist attacks was planned for September 22;

— a man caught in the explosion of one of the WTC towers rode bits of the falling building down to safety;

— an unburned Bible was found in the smoldering wreckage of the Pentagon.

One of the most striking example of bias in international coverage related to video images, broadcast by CNN, which indicated that some Palestinians were celebrating the September 11th events. The suspicion that the video was shot ten years ago was raised by a student in Brazil in a newsgroup; very quickly this message was spread through the internet.

There is absolutely no truth to the information that is now distributed on the Internet that CNN used a 10-year-old video showing the celebrating of some Palestinians in East Jerusalem after the terror attacks in the U.S. The video was shot that day by a Reuters camera crew. The CNN statement ends with the plea, to e-mail it "to anyone you now". On the positive side, the Internet was one of the main channels for communication after the attacks in New York, especially as a substitute for broken telephone connections. But the function of the Internet in terms of crisis communication was much broader.

Individuals have become part of the media flow as never before, as emailed articles, letters, rumours, investigative reports, personal stories, photos and videos fly around the Net. The free, open publishing system of the Independent Media Centres and alternative press aggregators like Alternet spread news and perspectives often absent from the mainstream press.

Peace advocates are developing their media strategies. Online communities, including MediaChannel's new Forum, are hosting insightful and often heated discussions. Crisis communication becomes multi-directional, more intercultural. If you compare coverage of the Gulf War and recent events in Afghanistan with the coverage of Kosovo war the differences are obvious: the lack of Internet resources in the first two cases was caused by a television-centered crisis communication with a high dependency on military information.

In the case of the Kosovo war, there were Internet-based information sources right where the war was occurring, from e-mail to Web sites, all of which reported as private correspondents and eyewitnesses. This multidirectional form of crisis communication allowed the audience to compare and evaluate different sources and to understand better the biases of official information.

Media communication is supplemented by personal communication personal journalism. The disembeddedness of Internet communication relative to time means that there is a continuous flow of information; news spreads without temporal boundaries. The network characteristics of the Internet enable distribution to an unlimited audience.

For example, only minutes after the first plane hit the north tower of the World Trade Center a message about that event appeared on a newsgroup (slashdot.org) together with a query to the group community for further information. The Internet also accelerated the distribution of several rumours, but also permitted clarification and correction. The Internet has become a watch dog of official and journalistic crisis communication. We have different examples of sites examining the coverage of the crisis between Israel and Palestine.

The Internet becomes a global archive of crisis communication. Much of the Kosovo coverage is still archived on the Web; for example, see the Global Policy Forum's Kosovo archives. In case of the September 11th events, Web sites around the world created archives as a kind of virtual memorial for those killed in the event; see for example September11News.com. For research in crisis communication these archives provide unique opportunities to compare different events and cases.

The Internet creates global virtual communities. These communities are different from those invented by traditional media and political interests. In these communities, individuals expressed their emotions and asked urgent questions often on a highly sophisticated level. "Because all of America was affected by the events of Sept. 11, the Internet and 24-cable news shows quickly assumed the role of electronic town halls.

But if those forms of communication initially brought the country together in displays of public grieving - through broadcasts of memorial services and Web site tributes to the victims - they have more lately become national forums for the expression of anxiety." The September 11th events demonstrated very clearly that media communication is inextricable interwoven in the crisis it self.

Media reporting about the crisis shape the picture of the crisis, and is itself a factor in the dynamics of the crisis. Much has changed since the earliest newspapers of centuries ago, where months would lapse between events and their reporting in the media. Today, thanks to real-time coverage, the event and the image of the event nearly fall together. That means that no one can deal with a crisis without taking into account its images. Indeed, the Spetember 11th events demonstrate a high degree of staging for the media.

The integration of the Internet in crisis communication alters the role of journalism and undermines the power of communication of official sources. What we can state is a loss of information control by journalists and official sources. As Jim Hall draws the consequences from the Kosovo crisis communication: "One of the roles of journalism in this ocean of information is to help readers negotiate the various impasses that arise around bad and contradictory information, even from reputable sources".

Journalists are no longer only the gatekeepers of information but they must become guides for global information space. Media which communicates the crisis becomes a factor of the crisis itself. We learned already from the Gulf War coverage that satellite TV can become a factor for the dynamics of the crisis itself - an observation we could make in the September 11th crisis as well.

For example when George Bush and Osama bin Laden used television for their messages, this was expected to influence the development of the crisis. But in a deeper sense this became true for the Internet: the terrorists used Internet communication to plan and to coordinate their attacks, made possible by the disembeddedness of the medium and the corresponding lack of communication control.

We have to consider in crisis communication that there are tendencies towards a global public. Satellite TV like CNN or Al Jazeera are the starting points of a global public. But with the Internet this becomes much more apparent. So whoever communicates in a crisis, which is of international relevance, has to be aware of a global audience. Of course one has to take into account that the access to Internet communication is far from a fair distribution in the different regions of the world.

There are multiple perspectives on crisis communication: This multiperspectivity of course includes all the errors, rumours, hoaxes, and false information. But on the other side stands an enrichment of public communication from more sources than just journalistic ones. "The Internet has been a godsend during the Kosovo crisis.

As a library, a specialized message board and a distribution method for dozens of non-traditional sources of information the medium has begun to fulfil its ballyhooed promises". The single citizen is much more responsible for his level and quality of knowledge than ever before. As trust and risk are, as stated above, subjective categories, the individual has to care for his or her information security. In a global information world, citizens can no longer delegate the risk associated with information to journalists and other professionals.

Every citizen has to become a professional in information security. This is not meant as a kind of neo-liberal statement according to the message that everybody is responsible for his own fate, independent of his capacities. It means that in particular the media has to care for the improvement of the competence of their audience. And Internet is a good tool for this task.

There is an important difference in crisis communication depending on where the crisis happens. If you compare the picture of the exploding South Tower of the World Trade Center to the MSNBC picture of U.S. attacks on Kabul, the difference is apparent at once. A crisis in the middle of a media society guarantees the full attention of all media causing a completely different dynamic of crisis communication.

This relates to for example the quality of the information, the density of the information and also the emotional concern of the audience. So even the chances of crisis communication are very unequal if one compares the media potential in a developed media society with the potential in a undeveloped or developing country.

4

# Media and Globalisation

The most significant development of the last two decades in international communication is the increasing concentration of mass media ownership within and across national borders. This process has been facilitated by a world-wide trend toward deregulation and privatization of the mass media.

Concentration of mass media ownership has had two significant implications for the ways news (and other cultural products) is assembled and disseminated world-wide: First, concentration of ownership and privatization of mass media has been accompanied by commercialization of news and other cultural products, a trend that is characterized by aesthetic, technical, and professional standardization at the global level.

And second, alliances between the international "media moguls" such as Rupert Murdoch and forces of political conservatism has led to increasingly "soft" media content. These phenomena are part of the process of globalization.

These trends in the political economy of international mass communication have left little space for information that questions the status quo, and even less space for material that forcefully advocates even limited structural change. A prevailing model of journalistic practice that emphasizes neutrality, "facts," authority, official expertise, and so on, has helped ensure that alternative views and oppositional voices remain largely unheard.

The widespread use of the prevailing model, the origins of which can be traced to the rise of a "professional" journalism in Europe and the United States, has aided the owners of mass media corporations in their world-wide expansion by ignoring or, at best, not fully analyzing important global developments such as the social, political, and cultural implications of the international corporate concentration of mass media firms. What consumers of mainstream mass media often are left with is generic news content that emphasizes titillation, sensational events, and politically "safe" topics.

Contextualized and critical discussions of social and economic trends, deep analysis of the human condition, and material that provides genuinely useful information for mass media consumers is often consigned to the back burner, if not the dust bin. Consequently, the potential for journalism to nurture and expand any semblance of civil society, a space relatively independent of the state and the market, where open discussion and debate about (for example) the terms of social organization, the direction of public policy, the bases of cultural identity can take place among individuals, organizations, and other interest groups, is undermined.

For example, because commercialized mass media need large audiences to survive financially, they may respond by eliminating political news or avant garde entertainment deemed by the owners to have the potential to displease certain segments of their audience. The result is that the range of issues discussed in the news is reduced. And when an issue or problem deemed acceptable is discussed, the range of acceptable perspectives on the issue also is relatively small.

Consumers of this kind of artificially narrow and perhaps irrelevant information may begin to feel increasingly alienated and disconnected from the civic life of their communities. They may develop a sense that they are without relevant, actionable information and, therefore, powerless to control the course of their own lives.

## International Mass Communication

Currently there are five major corporate players in international mass communication. These giants are News Corp., Disney/Cap Cities, Time Warner, Viacom, and TCI. In addition, two other "mini-giants," General Electric and Westinghouse have global ambitions. Of these seven firms, all but Viacom and TCI have major news components.

News Corp. is the owner of or significant partner in newspapers, television stations, and satellite broadcasting systems (including STAR TV and Sky TV) around the world. Disney/Cap Cities owns ABC. Time Warner's recent acquisition of Turner Broadcasting, which created and owns CNN, gives it a major international presence in news gathering and dissemination. General Electric owns NBC. and Westinghouse owns CBS. All of these mega-corporations but one are based in the United States; News Corp. is based in Australia.

There are several other significant players in the international mass media. Among them are Japan's Sony Corporation, France's Havas and Hachette, Germany's Bertelsman AG, Holland's Philips Corporation, and the emerging Globo of Brazil and Televisa of Mexico. Nevertheless, News Corp., Disney/Cap Cities, Time Warner, General Electric, and Westinghouse epitomize the trend toward the international concentration of ownership among mass media firms.

The growth of global mass media firms has been fueled by a parallel move toward deregulation and privatization of mass media organizations. This is most clearly evident in the broadcasting sector, which in many countries of the world had been maintained as nonprofit, public service, state supported entities.

As the forces of capitalism and entrepeneurship have emerged as the dominant model of economic organization, the state has receded as a regulator of the market place . This development has allowed the global media giants to enter into partnerships with dozens of national mass media firms around the world to produce, provide and/or disseminate news and entertainment to domestic markets.

Advances in satellite broadcasting has secured the presence of the giant mass media firms in the cultural and information market place of every region of the world. If the current trend continues, as McChesney and others have noted, the day when most of the world's entertainment and journalism is provided by, or at least is somehow connected to, one of global mass media firms is not far off.

Of course, this does not mean that every person in the world will consume identical news and entertainment products. The content will be linguistically tailored and otherwise culturally adjusted to serve specific regions by institutional and individual users at the local level. But the invariably pro-profit and market orientation of the firms, along with staunchly conservative political orientation of their owners, will mean that some views, perspectives, genres, etc., will be off limits.

For example, journalism that reveals the inherently undemocratic nature of capitalism would not be acceptable to News Corp.'s owner Rupert Murdoch and his powerful political allies such as Great Britain's former Prime Minister Margaret Thatcher, former US President Ronald Reagan, and most recently, US House of Representatives leader Newt Gingrich.

In short, as long as serious journalism is deemed unprofitable, it will take a back seat to the sensational, superficial, and "soft" news stories of the day. James Carey has described the prevailing model in the following way: "Journalism...is an industrial art. The inverted pyramid, the 5 W's lead, and associated techniques are as much a product of industrialization as tin cans." Essentially, this prevailing model emphasizes "objectivity" and neutral observation; letting the "facts" speak for themselves; and heavy use of officials and experts as sources and attributions. It is a model that results in journalism that describes events with little analysis, relies upon polls and statistics to show social trends but without providing historical context, and provides no vehicle of expression for ordinary people at the grass roots level.

It is precisely the type of journalism that serves the interests of the owners of the global mass media firms because it avoids asking deeper questions about the exercise of power, the dispensation of social justice, and the prospects for cultural survival. Raising these types of issues under the prevailing model of journalism is difficult because it would force the journalism profession to jettison the notion of neutral, detached, "industrial" reporting. As a result, the news consumer is confronted each day with a numbing array of stories about political scandals, celebrity divorces, natural disasters, "horse race" reporting of politics, official pronouncements, and so on.

Journalism of this type does not fulfill the role of journalism in modern participatory democracies in which people participate in jointly deciding the direction and nature of civic life. The type of news now produced by the application of the prevailing model of journalism does little to facilitate deliberation and discussion of pressing social concerns of the day among news consumers.

In fact, the prevailing model of journalism results in news that may distance news consumers from one another in that the news stories do not provide information relevant for decision making; a sense of how the information (assuming it was relevant to begin with) is related to deliberations about public affairs; or a recognition of shared values upon which to make decisions related to the civic life of the community.

## Media and Alternative Journalism

For journalism to assume a more meaningful social and civic role, it must do what the prevailing model does not allow. It must raise fundamental questions about power, social justice, and culture. This effort requires that whenever appropriate, journalists take a stand, actively interpret "facts," let ordinary people speak about their experiences, and make moral and ethical judgments about the nature of capitalism (and racism, sexism, homophobia, patriarchy, etc.). Such an approach requires specific reporting strategies that move away from the short-sighted, myopic definitions of news and how to cover it. Also, the idea of journalistic objectivity must be recognized as a myth and must be replaced by a view of journalistic work in which the reporter is an integral part of and involved in the community which he or she reports.

Such an approach would emphasize processes rather than discrete events, dynamic explanations rather than static descriptions, bottom-up rather then top-down flow of information, a wide range of sources rather than officials and experts, and an explicit commitment to social change rather than professed neutrality. Journalists would replace the dry, mechanical recitation of "facts" with evaluation and interpretation.

Clearly these tasks represent the rudiments of a very different model of journalism than the one prevailing world-wide. In the prevailing model the emphasis is on providing factual accounts of seemingly disconnected events drawing upon the words of officials and the legitimacy of science (experts, polls, statistics) as evidence to support the account. The primary purpose is to describe the event by recounting the "who, what, when, and where," and less frequently the "why" and "how" of the story.

In the emancipatory model, the emphasis is on understanding how apparently discrete events fit into ongoing processes. Journalists interpret the meaning and significance of the "facts of the case" rather than letting the facts speak for themselves. To understand the subject upon which they are reporting, the journalists rely not only on officials and experts but also on ordinary local people and their grounded knowledge about the situation. The purpose of their work is to provide an explanation of why the news is relevant and a cognitive "map" that attempts to illuminate the significance of the current historical moment.

While the prevailing model of journalism reports facts perceived to be the truth and makes a conscious effort to remain detached from the subject of the story, emancipatory journalism makes explicit efforts to promote reform and encourage social action. Emancipatory journalism can encourage action simply by providing information that makes people aware of services, opportunities, and problems that need attention.

Readers can then act immediately and personally on information salient to their needs. Emancipatory journalism also can encourage reform by, for example, keeping the problems related to development on the agendas of policy makers so that they may be forced to take action leading to emancipatory social change.

Emancipatory journalism reports news in a fashion that uses a holistic approach, is people-oriented, and emphasizes advocacy. The holistic approach implies a recognition that globalization is a process and not an event. The enormously complex interconnections and trajectories of globalization may contribute to feelings of alienation and anxiety for those living through the process.

Emancipatory journalism may counteract these forces by providing the cognitive mapping necessary to establish a sense of physical and cultural orientation to news consumers. Emancipatory journalism can, for example, compare the current conditions with similar processes in other regions or countries and point out the unique needs and accomplishments of the local community.

Emancipatory journalism can discuss current conditions in the context of their cultural relevance and historical significance; point out the cultural implications and consequences of change; assess how (and if) people's needs are being met; and propose culturally relevant models for future plans. The people orientation of emancipatory journalism can help facilitate reconstruction of cultural identities.

Through the broadly democratic dialogic and "bottom-up" nature of emancipatory journalism, local communities can develop a set of concepts and theories that provide the basis not only for understanding the contradictions of international capitalism, but also for critiquing them and proposing alternatives. The advocacy emphasis of emancipatory journalism helps to create, maintain, and strengthen a space for resistance with news that helps propose visions of the future that make significant the current battles for autonomy, integrity, and security.

In my journalism classes at the University of Wisconsin, I've incorporated various aspects of the emancipatory journalism model. There were three projects emphasizing emancipatory journalism and the pedagogical lessons learned from the experiences. The projects are: Voices from the Community, Small-Scale Public Journalism, and Total Community Coverage.

### *Voices from the Community*

This project was initiated by a local social service organization called Madison Urban Ministry (MUM). MUM had conducted content analysis of local newspapers and found largely unflattering coverage of Madison's minority and poor communities. For example, negative stories received bigger headlines and more prominence, while positive stories received smaller headlines and less prominence; few people living in the communities covered were used as sources; and there was little explanation for why things happen (i.e. little context, history, background, implications).

MUM contacted me to help formulate strategies to get the local press to improve their coverage of minorities and the poor. First, we assumed that if we made a story easier to cover for the journalists, he or she is more likely to cover the story. So we tried to figure out ways that could be done. We thought about deadline pressures, reporting routines, and so forth and came up with a project based on bottom-up reporting in which journalism students would gain experience with an alternative model of reporting and writing.

Essentially, MUM served as a clearinghouse for news story ideas and sources. Two journalism students canvassed various neighborhoods in Madison where many poor and minority residents live due to a variety of structural factors in the community, and found out what issues, ideas, concerns are of importance, and what people in the community had something to say about these ideas, issues and concerns.

The students then prepared press releases (or story "recipes") to send to the local news media. The recipes would contain (1) an overview of the issue or concern, (2) explain why it's important for the entire community to know and be concerned about the issue, and (3) suggest non-traditional sources to contact.

The local media would then use these ideas for news stories and send out their own reporters to cover the issues. The results were disappointing: Local news media were not very interested, and we did not get extensive cooperation from the communities. What we learned is that we did not do enough to prepare and educate the local news media or the communities about the purposes, goal, and mechanism of the project. However, the journalism students gained valuable exposure to a different way of doing journalism as well as valuable experience interacting with people and communities they otherwise may never meet.

### *Small-scale Public Journalism*

In this second attempt, we thought more carefully about our conceptual approach to the project and decided to think about it as an exercise in public journalism. The basic idea behind public journalism is to have news organizations purposefully use their resources and activities to educate and interest people in becoming more active citizens. To carry out this task, news organizations must capture and then report accurately what citizens think are the most pressing issues of the day (not what the experts think) and then provide a forum for anyone who wished to express views.

In this regard, the news organizations may sponsor public meetings at which the community voices its views, bring policy makers together to discuss public concerns, or merely open up an opinion section in which members of the community can express their views.

The entire model is not easily applied in the classroom (nor should it be, given some of its serious shortcomings), but the information gathering and reporting part of the model fruitfully can be used to teach students information-gathering techniques other than the standard journalistic interview, and to convey a sense that reporters can be connected to the Communities they report without sacrificing their professionalism. In this project, we first got a local newspaper to agree that it would run news stories written from the perspectives we were emphasizing. Then, after MUM representatives briefed community leaders about the project, a senior journalism honors student began to assess the community mood and priorities not through surveys and polls, but through ethnographic methods of observations and depth interviews (to tap into "grounded knowledge about" the community). He discussed what issues were at stake in the community through contact not only with officials but also community leaders and community centers. To help the student reporter develop a sense that he was part of the community, not a detached observer of it, he was encouraged to develop social contacts in the community; make personal visits; and help people compose and articulate their ideas for letters to the editor, etc.

This project was not completed at the time of this writing. So far the student reporter has made sustained contact with a local community center. Members of the community there and the journalism student are collaborating on developing story ideas, sources, and story formats for publication in the local newspaper that agreed to participate in the project.

### *Total Community Coverage*

The Maynard Institute for Journalism Education in Oakland California, developed this project in 1992. They send their team to newspapers that request the two-week seminar during which the concept of TCC is taught to the editorial staff. The concept is based on getting the editorial personnel to think of the whole community as its constituent; not just those people who the advertising department is after but the poor, youth, minorities, those on fixed income, the elderly, etc.

The entire community becomes the subject, sources, and market for the newspaper. The two-week seminar includes (1) content audit (an inventory of patterns in the news coverage of the newspaper: what topics are getting most emphasis, what sources are most frequently used); (2) presentation and workshops focusing on news gathering, combining words and images in news and advertising, blurring traditional boundaries of beats and reporting in teams, and new routines for cultivating news sources; (3) production of a special section for insert into regular publication containing the results of discussions on TCC; (4) community outreach meetings to gauge reader reactions to the TCC approach (especially to determine if TCC-based news forced readers to view community differently, and whether new kinds of social relationships formed across race, gender, class lines).

Again, each part of the TCC model is not applicable in journalism classrooms, but the concept of viewing the whole community as subjects and sources for news stories is consistent with emancipatory journalism and can be taught at all levels of the curriculum.

One of the most useful lessons students learn with this model is the blurring of lines between news beats, between "hard" news and analysis, and between reporter and community. Beats are no longer relevant because the whole community is the unit being reported in each story. The journalists learn that they can be a positive influence on the life of the community as they view their specific story from the perspective of the total community.

Children are immersed daily in a dense bath of mass media images and messages. Some teach children about the world around them. Some are miseducational and promote deceptive, partial, stereotypical and sometimes harmful perceptions. The Convention on the Rights of the Child recognizes the positive and negative influences of the media on children.

Article 17 of the Convention obligates governments to help ensure that mass media disseminates information for children that promotes their well-being, inclusive of physical, spiritual, moral and mental health. It also outlines children's right to actively access information that is of social and cultural benefit to them.

Article 17 states that governments must take steps to protect children from harmful information, and recognizes the crucial role of parental guidance in children's access to media and information. Article 34 reinforces children's right to protection from exploitation, including the sexually exploitative portrayal of children in the media.

Recognizing that children - particularly children of marginalized populations - are often completely invisible in the media, or are stereotyped as passive victims or as aggressors, children's rights to participation encourage the voice of children in the media. When children are consulted and active participants in creating media and information, their rights to survival, development and protection can be advanced.

When children have access to information on issues that directly concern them, they can form and express opinions and make responsible decisions for their health and well-being. Young people in developing countries are particularly vulnerable to being misrepresented by media in that they, for the most part, do not have access to the technology and therefore are not agents in creating images of themselves in the world.

Images of war and famine give children the idea that developing countries are in a constant state of deprivation and disaster. The mass media do little to explain the causes of extreme events, or depict the normal daily life of most people in developing countries.

## Interactive Device for Infoage

The combination of the personal computer with on-line services and the Internet is rapidly achieving the promise of ubiquitous information access for education and entertainment, electronic commerce, and work-at-home. While telephone companies position themselves to enter the television delivery business and cable companies attempt to provide telephone services, the foundation for the information age is actually being built by the computer industry.

Unfortunately, a widely-held belief that personal computers serve only a small, technically savvy, and wealthy elite coupled with concern that computers are too difficult for mere mortals to use has mistakenly put the spotlight on creating interactivity on the television. This, compounded with the fact that TVs are present in virtually every home, resulted in some erroneous conclusions. In fact, television was designed for one thing only: moving pictures. It is a poor device for handling the high-resolution static images required for a high degree of interactivity. With the possible exception of video games, it is primarily a passive device. The fact that there are so many TVs is not relevant. If it were, we would have long ago considered interactive radio.

The number of televisions has become a false beacon for media companies, communications companies, equipment suppliers, and government policy makers. Since the technological and social infrastructure for interactive television does not exist—and its creation would be a truly awesome task—government has stepped into the breach, preoccupying itself with fostering its existence, and getting involved in the processes by which it will evolve. Issues of interoperability standards, competitive markets, and universal access have become matters of public policy. This is further complicated by the fact that television and telecommunications services are regulated, implying the need for regulation of interactive television and, by implication, the information superhighway.

This approach of imposing the television as the interactive communication device standard is based on a set of mistaken assumptions. The fact is that the ubiquitous information device exists now in the form of the personal computer (PC). In fact, while the government and the telecommunications companies argue about how best to deregulate the telecom industry, consumers are voting with their pocketbooks by purchasing personal computers, the only available interactive information device, at record levels.

## PC: An ubiquitous Interactive medium

The role model for the diffusion of personal computers into society may well resemble the adoption of the automobile. Business to a large extent is underwriting both the investment in developing the networks (the role the government had to play in developing the highway system for the automobile) and, very importantly, the training of a large number of consumers in the use of computers.

Telephone and cable companies have been regulated for most of their existence. As a result, they are well positioned to influence government policy with respect to the information superhighway. The computer industry, on the other hand, has had almost no regulation and has had little to no involvement with government. Those of us in the computer industry need to do our part in demonstrating to our policy makers that the information superhighway is already under construction. It is being built primarily on PC technology by private industry, driven by competitive market forces, and with little, if any, need for government regulation.

There is a role for government, however—to recognize and embrace the personal computer. This can provide us with a foundation for the next century that will not only improve the quality of our lives, but also improve the productivity of our society and the competitiveness of our industries. The government can do many things to move this along. It can facilitate access to computing in schools, libraries, and community centers. It can become one of the largest (maybe the largest) content provider of on-line information. It can encourage business to promote telecommuting. The most important thing the government can do is to recognize what is happening. However, we caution against interference with market forces. The market moved the personal computer industry forward at a phenomenal pace, and we encourage following this model rather than the heavily-regulated telecommunications model that has proven slow to evolve and respond.

Today, the primary use of personal computers is in business. It is interesting to note that it was originally conceived as a consumer product. The first personal computers were designed for either hobbyists or for consumers. Even IBM broke with its tradition of providing business products when it introduced the PC in 1981. This machine, which is the ancestor of over 85% of the computers sold today, actually had a game port for joysticks and an audio cassette for storage. Industry leaders at the time, such as Ken Olsen, then CEO of Digital Equipment Corporation, openly referred to personal computers as istoys. Few realized that these toys would completely restructure the entire computer industry within 10 years.

The personal computer overtook the mainframe with its terminals as the information tool of business sometime during the 1980s. It is interesting to note that, although there are clear reasons for this success, the mainframe was not without its merits. As a centralized facility, a mainframe is easy to control. Each user has access to the same software, and support is easy. Another clear advantage of main-frames is that, since they are a shared commodity, it is easy to manage capacity to match the average expected load. On the other hand, under peak usage, all users typically experience slower performance.

Probably, the main reason for the rapid decline of the mainframe, however, is the slow pace of progress in both hardware and software performance. While there are many reasons for the success of the PC in business, the most important is its evolutionary nature. The hopenness of the PC allowed for rapid innovation. The open bus inspired hardware companies to add value to the basic PC. They experimented in the marketplace. Successful additions were then integrated into the main computer. It is hard to imagine that the first PC had a built-in game port, while the printer port was optional. Application software could be created by small companies.

Companies like Lotus and WordPerfect grew from one product, while Microsoft took an early lead in the operating system and Novell provided the next work environment. While this environment was, and still is, chaotic, it provided for rapid evolution. No industry or government organization dictated the direction or set the standards, yet standard interfaces evolved out of economic necessity. The customers reward companies for innovation. When a company won in the market, others would accept its standard as the de facto standard and would seek to integrate their products into it. In the process, the personal computer became the tool of business. The adoption of personal computing into business in the United States was rapid.

Electronic mail has followed word-processing and spreadsheets as a key business application. This has made the PC a fundamental communication device. While e-mail has historically been used within a company, more and more companies are using it as a way of communicating with the outside world (customers, vendors, and partners). Now, many individuals are finding that they can also send notes to friends and relatives.

The term 'social computing' is gaining currency. A poor term no doubt, but a powerful concept. And while standards bodies were formed to address the methods by which different electronic mail systems would communicate, the Internet became the lingua franca of e-mail. Now, as businesses connect to the Internet to send and receive mail, they are also discovering that they can access a wide variety of information there as well. More and more companies are beginning to use the World Wide Web to communicate with the outside world. The growth of the Internet is staggering. It is estimated that, at the present moment, 10,000 companies are adding their presence to the Internet each week.

The growth of computing in the home has been a surprise even to those in the industry. In the early 1990s, a critical mass of home PCs equipped with modems enabled an explosion in a new industry: the on-line marketplace. Customers are now finding that much of the value of having a personal computer resides in the ability to connect with other users and with a large number of on-line services.

Although over 30% of U.S. homes are already equipped with PCs (a ramp faster than many consumer electronic products), the growth shows no sign of slowing down. On the contrary, with other countries joining in, worldwide shipments of PCs are expected to grow from 60 million units in 1995 to over 100 million by the year 2000.

The power of today's computer is mind-boggling by the standards of just a decade ago. The typical computer being purchased has a powerful microprocessor (typically, a Pentium) with computing power equal to the mainframe of just six years ago. This, combined with a high-resolution display, a CD-ROM, and CD-quality audio sound provides for a rich multimedia experience. Todays PC uses compression to display video that matches the quality of a typical VCR with only 0.5% of the information required for an analog video stream. The decompression of the data is performed in the microprocessor without any specialized hardware. In addition to this, it can act as a fax machine and provide access to on-line networks and the Internet. It is used for a variety of purposes from entertainment to education, work-at-home, and home shopping.

The capabilities of the personal computer are improving at a rate no other device has ever experienced. Historically, the power of a PC has doubled every 18 months. This rate has recently increased, and the capabilities are doubling every 12 months. What will we do with such computing power? Here are some of the most obvious areas:

— Improvements in ease of use, including natural language input and output.

— Powerful 3-D graphics.

— Outstanding audio/video capabilities.

— Video telephony.

— Multitasking (doing several things at the same time).

Historically, the computer industry was vertically integrated. Computer companies did everything from designing their own power supplies to developing application software. Each vertical stack was unique and proprietary. The PC changed all that. The PC industry is basically horizontal, with literally thousands of companies delivering compatible products, at every level of integration, and in many areas of applications. The result of the horizontal nature of the computer industry is fierce competition at every level along both quality and price. This competition benefits customers who have access to the performance at the lowest prices. De facto interfaces have emerged at the intersection of the various segments. Periodically, ad hoc industry groups are formed to cooperate in creating new interfaces. An example is the PCI bus, which has become the standard for the high-speed internal bus of personal computers.

The cable television industry still operates in the traditional vertical organization. Cable companies are the only suppliers of both equipment and services, and most consumers don't even have the opportunity to buy their own equipment. As a result, equipment is typically not interoperable between different companies, technical progress is slow, and prices do not decline. This slow progress, in turn, stands in the way of improvements in other parts of the value delivery chain. As a result, government has recently stepped in to regulate both function and price.

## Difference between TV and PC

Televisions use CRTs to display moving pictures, as do most personal computers. This fact sums up the essential similarity between these two devices. The fact is that in their purpose, their features, their evolution, in the way they are sold, and, perhaps most important, in the way they are used and are connected to the outside world, televisions and personal computers have very little in common.

The television was designed to bring visual entertainment, from the movie theatre and the stage, into the home. This emphasis on the visual is seen, for example, in the fact that, until recently, the quality of television speakers was far below that of other consumer electronics devices and that, even today, few programs are broadcast in stereo. To its credit (depending on your point of view), the television also enabled some new forms of entertainment such as game shows and brought us news footage. A common element to all these experiences is that they are typically enjoyed in the family room, from a comfortable distance, in a reclined position. The PC, on the other hand, was originally designed as a work tool and a platform for gaming. Two of the first applications exist on the PC were the Lotus 123 spreadsheet and Microsoft's Flight Simulator. Although these applications would seem to be very different, they both required the user to sit close to the PC and to interact with it on a continuous basis (whether the device used is a keyboard or a joystick is not important).

The NTSC standard for television broadcast in the United States specifies 483 lines of video. In practice, most broadcasts and most VCRs are only capable of about half of that. By contrast, the minimum resolution for any personal computer monitor sold today is 1024 ¥ 768, with many exceeding that. There are many reasons that explain the poor resolution of televisions—the most significant being that it is adequate for the purpose at hand, and the cost of upgrading the system is huge. But resolution is only one of the differences. Probably much more crucial the fact that the PC is inherently an intelligent device capable of processing information locally and of interacting directly with the user. The PC also has local storage that can be used for programs, data, video, or whatever the user thinks is important.

The single-most important difference between the TV and the PC has nothing to do with any one feature but with the fact that the PC is constantly changing, in effect adding features on a regular basis. For those who live in the world of telecommunications and television where things move very slowly (witness ISDN and HDTV), the PC hyper-growth may be difficult to comprehend.

Now that HDTV is being proposed, the TV is being asked to do something it has not done in 40 years: evolve. Televisions have remained fundamentally the same, with the exception of screen size, since the introduction of colour TV almost 40 years ago (even that change was a very painful one that resulted in a compromise that still hurts the picture quality of television). While some features have been added to the television, and the VCR gave it a limited linear memory, most new features are seldom used.

### *Interactivity*

Interactivity can be defined as an activity where individuals are fully engaged in a process. Interaction is something that involves an interplay between people or between people and devices such as a computer. We wish to contrast that to control and navigation. While there may be a brief moment or two where we interact with our remote control and TV in order to select a program of interest, success usually means long stretches of passive involvement with the program of choice. While the telephone can be used for some form of interactive information retrieval or even to perform a transaction by using the keys and following a menu of choices, most would agree that this is not a very enjoyable experience, and it is not suitable for sustained periods of time. This should be contrasted with the PC, a device with which individuals routinely interact for hours at a time.

### *Connectivity*

The TV was built from the start to be a communications device—albeit one-way communications. After all, a TV without a connection to the outside world is useless. In fact, it is the television network, especially cable, rather than the TV itself, that has expanded to offer more services. So it is this paradigm that has motivated the communications companies to approach the problem of providing interactive service to consumers in a similar way. It is therefore very ironic that the PC, which gave users the independence to work on their own and to break away from the mainframe, is, in fact, the superior communications device. This is because, on the PC, which is capable of producing, processing, and storing information, communications evolved from the very start as a two-way interaction.

The TV is only easy to use if it is used in its simplest form. To make the TV more intelligent in order to be interactive, something has to be added to it. This is typically called an intelligent set-top box. The idea is to add to the TV many of the functions of the personal computer and the game machine—but at a price that is consistent with television pricing (typically, $300 is the target). Since $300 does not buy a lot of computing power, much of the intelligence needs to be somewhere else in the network where it can presumably be shared. If this sounds familiar, it is because it copies the mainframe/dumb terminal concept. The computer industry has the advantage of having seen that movie and of being familiar with its pitfalls. Since the intelligent PC was so successful in replacing the mainframe 10 years ago, there is no need, this time, to go through the same steps.

## The Telephone Industry

Much of what was said about the television is also true of the telephone. This device, too, has been slow to evolve (touch-tone being the last, and probably first, breakthrough in the device itself). Here, too, it is the network which is responsible for most innovations such as 800 service and call waiting. The awaited breakthrough on the telephone side (equivalent to HDTV) has been some form of video telephony. All attempts have failed because the cost and quality have not been there. On the other hand, personal computers have offered video telephony incorporating application sharing, on ISDN for some time. It is expected that the personal computer's current trajectory will allow it to offer a marketable quality video telephony product over POTS within the current year with the simple addition of a camera.

As the television and telephone industries eye each other's heartland but consider the massive cost of doing battle with each other, they each hope to create an advantage by offering a new class of service: interactive TV services. Unfortunately, they both have a poor track record in evolving their businesses. And this time, they must build their new infrastructures in a matter of years—not decades.

How Will the PC Become Ubiquitous?

At the current rate of purchase, between 50% and 60% of homes will have computers by the end of the decade. While that is an amazing penetration, the other 40% needs to be addressed. This group can be broken up into those who would like to have a computer at home and those who have no interest. There is an obvious economic barrier facing a portion of those who would like to own a computer. Similarly, while most everyone has access to public transportation, not everyone owns a car. We strongly believe that access to the information highway via PCs will be made available to all people via computers at schools, community centers, libraries, and other government and private sites where the cost is spread over many users.

This economic barrier should not be construed as an opportunity for the television to evolve into interactive television. We believe that the cost of interactive TV (both the device itself and the network) would limit its availability to pockets of high income families. Since the PC is a multifunction device, its cost is, in fact, less of an obstacle—as can be seen by its fast ramp so far.

The following key characteristics of the personal computer industry ensure that the PC will continue to be the primary interactive device of the information superhighway:

— It is a highly-capable device designed from the start for interactivity.

— Its adaptability allows for rapid market experimentation, with the market setting the standard.

— Businesses have invested trillions of dollars in a computer infrastructure.

— Consumers, in turn, have benefited from this investment in the form of training, cheaper equipment, and access to infrastructure.

— The Internet, which is the only national information infrastructure, was specifically built for and with computers and is a common network for business and consumers.

The first requirement is an access point with an interactive device. By this, we refer to interactivity as defined by the current and evolving personal computers, as opposed to improvements in the navigation and control capabilities of TV. We assume that PCs will not only become easier to use, but will be able to handle rich media (video, audio, and images, in addition to text), with better and better quality. Next, we need a communications infrastructure that connects these access points to services and to each other. This connection must provide adequate bandwidth in order to enable the use of rich, multimedia data types.

The current POTS environment, even with the latest 28.8 Kb/s data rate, is extremely limiting. ISDN is a short- and intermediate-term opportunity to increase bandwidth to the consumer. Over time, broadband capabilities will be needed. It should be noted that bandwidth symmetry is not required as long as adequate bandwidth is available in the return path. For example, the current PC-to-cable connection experiments, while highly asymmetric in bandwidth, would be quite adequate for accessing existing Internet sources. Clearly, we will need higher bandwidth in the return path if we are to expand beyond current modes of use and allow every user to become a contributor of rich data.

The governments should:

— Recognize that the PC is the interactive device and that the Internet is the Information Superhighway. they are the closest in satisfying our future needs. Furthermore, they are open standards with industry momentum behind them; they are the winners of the Darwinian process of evolution.

— Encourage employers to make work-at-home a major thrust. Telecommuting will have economic, social, and environmental benefits. It will also provide computers at home for many who might not be able to afford them otherwise.

— Develop programs making networked computers available to all via schools, community centers, and other government facilities. L Encourage a competitive communications environment with specific advantages to those who provide the low-cost, two-way, high bandwidth required by personal computers at home.

— Avoid trying to set standards or dictate economic behaviour. Also, avoid any procedures that slow down the creation of de facto market-developed standards.

— The government should encourage states and municipalities to deregulate the local loop so that advanced telecommunications services can be more readily available to the consumer. ISDN, for instance, should not be looked upon as something for the techno-rich, but as a service available to all.

— Finally, capitalizing on the enormous amount of information it collects, but has not been able to redistribute efficiently, the government should become a major provider of content and services on the Internet.

Marshall McLuhan prophesied the information age in his 1960's book, *Understanding Media*. He suggested that to understand technology, we should look at it in a different way. Briefly, McLuhan's theory addresses the process of projection. As human beings, we "project" aspects of ourselves into our creations whether art, technology, social organizations, spiritual paradigms, in effect, the way we see the world. Through the mirror of our world, we know who we are. Our industrial age machines and things, production design, business procedures, and what we choose to bless as worthwhile social values are a projection of our preoccupation with our physical body's bones, muscles, actions, reactions, and desires.

During the information age, our creations, our technologies, our social structure, and our values become a reflection of our preoccupation with, not only our physical nervous system, but with our cognitive processes. This includes analysis, reflection, awareness, feelings, consciousness and other mysterious "things" of human experience that "mechanistic" psychologists try to "nail down" with stick-pins on the walls of their industrial psychology factories. In order to handle the information age conceptually, it is not enough to simply change our perspective from mechanistic to processional, from thing orientation to human orientation. What is required is a shift in consciousness about who we are as human beings and, therefore, every aspect of our lives.

The cognitive process is multidimensional, perhaps beyond the four dimensions of time and space. There is no single first step or linear path for our logical mind to follow but a complex of many connections and relationships. The multidimensional nature of cognition is also the reason interactive programs are more effective for education, training, or motivation. Involvement process, as well as data, enhances memory retention and understanding.

Let's look at a portion of the cognition process specific to our perspective on "information." Information specialists are now considering information as a process rather than a "thing." Data is not information. Information must have meaning. Human consciousness gives meaning to data. We take data and organize it into a form that is useful to humans. That usefulness may be for understanding, work performance, or recreation. The form and order we put data into may have several connecting paths that are linear, a productivity workflow in a training video or as a story line in a movie. Nevertheless, the paths eventually must describe a multidimensional whole, a context that enables the human mind to reason for meaning and purpose.

The task of the creative person in the communications professions is to provide the form of the communication with all the context of meaning, purpose, inter-activity, and relatedness. Some of the elements are composition, action, story line, continuity, rhythm, mood, tone, and colour. The form constructed by these elements' relationships establishes meaning. The creation is a reflection of the creator's conscious and unconscious cognitive processes.

Looking at information from a cognitive, human point of view is just one perspective of "The" paradigm shift! Let's shift perspective and look at the social-political context of the Information Age. Communication requires an exchange of relevant and organized data from person(s)-to-person( s). The traditional industrial age mind-set would see data moving from point A to point B in a linear process. This mind-set is based on political, social, and historical paradigms that are in the process of transformation.

In an industrial age society, information is centralized with controlled distribution - a hierarchical distribution Communication is a top-down, one way, one-to-many process just like the social and political structure. In traditional industrial companies or corporations, information is transferred from the boss to the workers in the form of dictatorial orders. The "need to know" rules inter-company and intra-company control of communication. In the typical case, information is filtered and even distorted on its way down the chain of command. As we all know from experience, the "chain of command" is not the only channel of information. The "grape vine" provides a functional anarchy, whether it is mouth-to-mouth, phone-to-phone, or client-to-client (computer talk).

Another example of hierarchical distribution is broadcast media. Television and radio broadcasts from networks, cable, and direct satellite are also one-way, one-to-many. In our democratic culture, we at least have multiple hierarchical broadcast systems, but it is important to notice that they are, nonetheless, hierarchical. Although broadcast is near universal in our culture, we really do have limited choices in what news and entertainment we receive. More choices cost more money. Cable television customers are still in the minority.

Our telephone system has always been democratic and, in recent years, universal. The telephone allows one-to-one and interactive (two-way) communication. You can call and talk to Mom and she can respond to you. Conference calls (many-to-many) are possible but are used mainly in the corporate world. The telephone and the automobile changed our society and our daily lives because both were universally accessible. Despite the high purchasing cost for an individual and despite government regulations of the highways and airways, these technologies have increased our freedom to move, communicate, and make a living. Barring a return to some form of dictatorial society or a general economic depression, there is no reason to predict that the merging of digital technologies into the Internet will have a reverse affect.

The Internet is ordered (or chaotic, depending on your control philosophy) in an interactive network of one-to-one, one-to-many, and many-to-one. This "digital soup" is very democratic (or anarchical). The legislative battle over de-regulation and monopoly control of the telecommunications industry is about how free and universal Internet access will be. Like the telephone system, the Internet is one-to-one and interactive. Unlike the telephone, the instruments of the Internet allow for broadcasting, one-to-many. If you merge the television broadcast metaphor with the telephone metaphor, you get an idea of the possible connections.

Marshall McLuhan said that if you merge two technologies into a hybrid, you would create a major transformation in society. This merging creates not just the results of 1 + 1 = 2 but is like a marriage: 1 + 1 = 3 (a child or other results of the creative act). Actually, more than two technologies are merging into this digital soup: television, radio, telephone, faxing, cellular phones, beepers, networked computers, portable computers, wireless phones and computers, and satellite transmissions.

When a hybrid technology forms from multiple technologies, new processes are created. The concept of "many-to-one" is one of these processes that may have very significant effects in the future. For example, there is a software metaphor called an "agent." An agent is like a robot that is able to travel self-directed all over the Internet. It gathers references and data that is relevant or customized to the customer (you, maybe) then reports to the customer on some schedule. Therefore, in effect, many sources of information travel to one. Many-to-one.

The form of the Internet has evolved into a wholistic or holographic process. Every part is connected to the whole (one-to-many) and the whole is connected to every part (many-to-one). In database management terminology, this is a "many-to-many" relationship and is only possible with "relational" database structure involving a third element that defines the "relationship" between the two other. Because of this technical structure, any individual can create a network of connections somewhat similar to the way a neuron in our brain "grows" connections as we grow from experience and knowledge.

The Internet can be considered a living entity made up from many living entities. The Internet is not only emulating the current psychophysical model of human mind/brain, it is beginning to emulate social consciousness. As we approached the Presidential elections of 1996, political parties and lobby groups were rushing to the Internet to establish home page presence, newsgroups, and chat groups focused on political issues and candidates. We may discover that the Internet media will be just as significant to the outcome of elections as the broadcast media has in the past. Through the Internet, we will all get more than the "pulse" of the public. As digital technology expands throughout the world, information access will become more difficult to control. The forces of traditional hierarchical control and the evolution of a truer democratic model of access will be at odds.

### *Advertisers and consumers*

Advertisers and consumers have had a relationship like men and women in our culture. The male (advertiser) was expected to do the courting and the woman (consumer) was expected to act like Sleeping Beauty (couch potato) and wait for someone interesting to come along. A customer with any discrimination could die in passivity while waiting for someone to offer something of value.

The customer is learning a little self-respect and is aggressively shopping for what she wants rather than what's offered up by the suitor. Consequently, she is snubbing uninvited, loud-mouthed, clowns who haven't a clue. Look at the early days of advertising -let's say, post-World War II. Before technology provided a path into the suburban home (a woman's domain despite the male castle fantasy), door-to-door salesmen (and they were all men) would knock on the suburban door and the housewife would actually welcome the visitation, perhaps expecting flowers. Who can blame her for wanting the outside world to enter her cloistered tower? At least, in those days, salesmen were gentlemen with manners. Then, when the telephone, radio, and TV became a path to reach her (the consumer), she began to expect the world to come to her with bright lights, colors, and music to woo her attention and flatter her unashamedly.

Maybe part of the evolution in consciousness has to do with technology empowering the individual with self-determining information and entertainment acquisition. Nevertheless, the larger context is about control. Our passive consumer market is changing into a truly consumer driven market. Nowadays, we, both men and women working in the world, have more need for privacy, seclusion, and safety at home and in our growing awareness of "personal space." Still, telemarketers ring the phone at dinner time, the fax machine beeps, and 150 plus TV channels plug into our private space with varying social etiquette, if any manners at all. In self-defense, we have to wake up and take control of our homes and our lives. Therefore, we take the option for Caller ID and answer machines. We schedule our kitchen and bathroom trips for commercial breaks or we sometimes turn the TV off to read a book or surf the Internet on our home computer. We are becoming more self-determined in choosing what information we need and we are more willing to make the effort to find it. Technology helps. We insist that information, when it gets into our face, be relevant to our individual needs. We want to define the value, too.

Somebody is buying the new technology, because deals are being made and empires are being fought over in the world of telecommunications and information management. Corporate giants in all industries and even political parties are buying territory along the information highway; some thinking, with unchanged paradigms, that business will be as usual. If they're still expecting to invade our homes with dominator style, rape, and plunder marketing strategies, they're in for a rude awakening themselves.

Basic etiquette cannot be designed or enforced by formal social laws. Enforcement comes from peer pressure and social consensus. Perhaps, in our present society, we do what we can "get away with." Actually, our ethics come from our deepest values and our values come from our deepest concept of how we feel about ourselves in our immediate social context.

Our values are not changing because of technology but because of a larger social transformational context.

The nature of the American Life was made possible by the evolution of a democratic society in which equality became an achievable goal. The ideal that an individual has inalienable rights is just a glimpse of the change in how we treat each other. The controversial question opens the possibilities for change. Human rights continue to be redefined in our culture and all over the world. Abuse is now defined on a psychological level as well as physical. Race, religion, and gender are no longer conditional qualifiers of individual justice. Yes, technology has become a major factor in this change. Certainly, universal and equal access to information and intellectual exchange increases the potential for social transformation. It does not predetermine the results. It calls the question.

Ideally, the sender/receiver and the receiver/sender must both be human and have a real time connection. Both must have respect for the ability and right of the other to contribute goods, information, knowledge, and wisdom. A dominator/victim attitude on either side contaminates the interchange. Demographic stereotypes, sexual, racial or social status conceptually limits the identity of the participants and set up the relationship for manipulation, competitiveness, and a win/lose results. Without a win/win process, the communication becomes unproductive.

Technology has made it difficult to "preach to" a captive audience. A free market continues to erode monopolies in products, service, information, and ideology. Each of us, as consumers has an expanding resource of options. As technology and commerce expands across national boundaries, citizens of the world will have more choices in what, where, when, and from whom they "buy" necessities of life, be they material or conceptual.

Equality and universality are paradigm shifts that have dramatically influenced one-to-one, personal relationships in the context of marriage and family. Recently, concepts of intimacy are being introduced in business, corporate culture, social, and political groups, now referred to as "communities." One of the concepts is partnering. This is a relationship that requires personal values or character ethics such as interdependence, win/win attitude, honesty, disclosure, vulnerability, and compassion, just to mention a few. People today are just tired of being treated generically, like statistics, in personal relationships, or in business.

The context of advertising and other commercial exchanges is no exception for the individual, enlightened consumer. We demand that people we have contact with, face-to-face or through technology, acknowledge and respect our privacy, our freedom of choice, our unique needs and desires, and our tradable goods: money, job productivity, skills, talents, experience, and wisdom. We also want to be acknowledged as whole persons - body, mind, and spirit.

The dominator/victim paradigm assumes that one side of the communication has control of all the resources (product, information, experience, and wisdom) and the other side is passive and has nothing to contribute. This is not true even if the trainee or student has no direct experience with the information at issue. As we are changing how we see others, and ourselves we realize that all humans bring their life experience and creativity to the situation and have much value to contribute. No matter how much expertise we have previously invested in our information or process, it is open to innovation from the people who participate in its implementation in the real world.

When the dominator attitude of one side defines their product or service as an inevitable choice of the other side, they are vulnerable to surprise. The customer has choices or will soon have choices from competitive products. The customer may not need the product at all. The customer may even become a producer of that same product. If the seller devalues the contribution of the consumer's money or resource, the exchange becomes a win/lose situation. A win/lose exchange is a temporary relationship. It can't last over the long haul. It will end when the loser runs out of resource for exchange or decides to buy somewhere else.

The Industrial Revolution provided the have-nots with more things for a higher standard of living. The Information Revolution promises to put more information in the hands of the now have-nots. The have-nots will continue to be empowered with a flourishing self-esteem and, consequently, an appreciation of all living beings.

# 5

# Digital Convergence

Life is becoming digital for some time now, We are surrounding ourselves with gadgets and we are consuming immense amounts of information, that is increasingly being delivered to us via the Internet. We play games, watch too much television and may be even looking forward to watch television on their mobile phone.

In november 2000, a theme issue of *the Scientific American* appeared, featuring a number of articles discussing (digital) entertainment in the era of digital convergence. It notes that the barriers between TV, movies, music, videogames and the Internet are crumbling. Audiences are getting new creative options. Moreover, it was observed that:

— digitizing everything audio and video will disrupt the entertainment industry's social order.

— the whole concept of holding a CD or movie in your hand will disappear once d-entertainment is widely available.

Underlying the importance of entertainment in the era of digital convergence is the premise governing an entertainment economy, which may be stated as there is no business without show business.

In that same issue of the *Scientific American* Gloria Davenport, a pioneer in the field of multimedia, presents list of applications characterizing the evolution of digital entertainment,

— 1953: interactive television, drawing exercise

— 1972: ping-pong on computer screen

— 1977: text-based interactive fiction

— 1983: laser-disc technology 3D game

— 1989: interactive simulation game

— 1989: the Ride

— 1993: 3D action game

— 1995: interactive web-based soap opera

— 1999: back to Atlantis

— 2000: TV + around the clock Web watch + voting

— 2001: fun enhanced web sites

The list compiled by Gloria Davenport suggests, a convergence towards an 'ultimate digital experience'. Considering the variety of means we have at our disposal to communicate, as reected in the list below, we may wonder whether our current technology really stands out as something special.

— *oral*: communicate symbolic experiences

— *writing*: record symbolic experiences

— *paper*: portability
— *print*: mass distribution
— *telegraph*: remote narrow communication
— *telephone*: remote analog communication
— *radio*: analog broadcasting of sound
— *television*: analog A/V broadcasting
— *recording media*: analog recording
— *digital processing*: machine enhancement
— *internet*: multimedia communication

Internet-based multimedia communication differs from earlier communication technology in that it somehow frees the message from the medium. Now, the Internet allows the synthesis and rendering of information and experiences using whatever is the most appropriate media to convey the message. The message is just the message, and the medium is just the medium. From a technological perspective there seems to be no limit, except those imposed by our own phantasy

## Cyberspace

The notion of cyberspace was introduced in William Gibson's novel Neuromancer, that appeared in the early 1980's, signifying a vast amount of (digital) data that could be accessed only through a virtual reality interface that was controlled by neuro-sensors. Accessing data in cyberspace was not altogether without danger, since data protection mechanisms (including firewalls, as we call them nowadays) were implemented using neurofeedback. Although the vision expressed in Neuromancer is (in our days) still futuristic, we are confronted with a vast amount of information and we need powerful search engines and visualisation techniques not to get lost.

On reflection, our (electronic) world of today might be more horrendous than the world depicted in Neuromancer. In effect, cyberspace television, video cassettes, video tape-recorder/players, video games, and personal computers all form an encompassing electronic system whose various forms interface to constitute an alternative and absolute world that uniquely incorporates the spectator/user in a spatially decentered, weakly temporalized and quasi-disembodied state.

All these gadgets make us dizzy, stoned with information and fried by electromagnetic radiation. However, the reality of everyday computer use is less exciting than the images in Neuromancer suggest. User interfaces are usually tiresome and not at all appealing. So except for the fanatic, the average user does easily get bored. Would this change when virtual reality techniques are applied pervasively? What is virtual reality? virtual reality virtual reality (is) when and where the computer disappears and you become the 'ghost in the machine'... In other words, virtual reality is a technology that provokes immersion, sensuous immersion, supported by rich media and powerful 3D graphics. In our age of information, we may wonder how all that information should be presented.

## Convergence

Let's see if we are able to give a more precise characterization of digital convergence. In their introduction to the theme issue of *the Scientific American,* Forman and SaintJohn locate the beginning of digital convergence, historically, at the 1939 New York World Fair. They observe that the receiver at the RCA Pavillon was way ahead of its time, it was a combination of television - radio - recorder - playback - facsimile - projector. Moreover, they remark that in hindsight suggests that we humans have a fundamental desire to merge all media in one entity By way of definition we may state, following Forman and SaintJohn, that digital convergence is: digital convergence the union of audio, video and data communication into a single source, received on a single device, delivered by a single connection And, as they say, predicted for decades, convergence is finally emerging, albeit in a haphazard fashion.

Taking a somewhat closer look, we may discern subsidiary convergences with respect to content, platform and distribution:

— *content*: audio, video, data

— *platform*: PC, TV, internet, game machine

— *distribution*: how it gets to your platform

Here, Forman and SaintJohn remark that if compatibility standards and data protection schemas can be worked out, all d-entertainment will converge into a single source that can shine into your life on any screen, whereever you are..

It is fair to say that no device has changed the way we live so dramatically as television. Television, for one, has altered the way we furnish our living rooms, not to speak about the time we waste watching the thing. Now, we may wonder what interactive television and enhanced television have to offer us. Looking back, we may observe that it takes some time for the new possibilities to catch on. For example, although many people watched Big Brother when it first appeared on television, the willingness of the audience to react other than by phone was (apparently) somewhat disappointing. Perhaps, in the Netherlands this was due to the fact that only a fraction of the PC owners was, at that time, permanently online.

Nevertheless, Forman and SaintJohn state, somewhat optimistically, that the convergence of digital content, broadcast distribution and display platforms create the big convergence of d-entertainment and information with feedback supporting human interactivity.

### *Digital television*

Currently, there are some (competing) standards in development, that will enable the mass-scale adoption of digital television, notably:

— VSB (vestigial side-band): not for antennas

— COFOM (coded orthogonal frequency): antennas, cable, satelite

When speaking about (digital) television, we must make a further distinction between:

— HDTV: high definition television

— SDTV: standard definition television

— ITV: interactive television

Will we prefer to watch stored video, instead of live television broadcasts? Will the Internet be able to compete with traditional television broadcasting. Will

Delay TV or Replay-TV, which allows you to watch previous broadcasts at a time that suits you become popular? Will an extended game machine or PC replace your television? Currently, we must observe that streaming media (still) have rather poor resolution. Leaving game machines aside, will it then be the TV or PC that will become our platform of choice? Forman and SaintJohn observe:

The Entertainment TV might make sense to adopt a programmable PC that can support competing TV standards, rather than construct a stack of TV peripherals. Nevertheless, there are a number of problems that occur when we (collectively) choose for the PC as our platform for d-entertainment:

— thin clients (Sun/Java) vs fat clients (MS/Intel:Dell,Compaq)

— Internet (IP) is not robust — QoS

— proprietary architectures and codecs — RealVideo, QuickTime, Windows media

Convergence with respect to distribution will not result in one single way of being connected, but rather a range of options from which one will be selected transparently, dependent on content and availability.

One possible scenario, not too unlikely after all, is to deploy it for installing computing devices everywhere, to allow for ubiquitous computing

— smart houses,

— smart clothes, and even

— a smart world.

## Technological Determinism

Although there are many technical issues involved in (digital) multimedia, as exemplified in the issues that play a role in digital convergence, a technical perspective alone does not suffice. Each technological innovation has its consequences on our social life. Conversely, each trend in society might result in the adoption or development of new technology.

Media as materials each medium of communication tended to create a dangerous monopoly of knowledge. For example for Christians, images where both a means of conveying information and a means of persuasion, that is part of the rethorics of institutionalized religion. Looking at our age, and the media that have come into existence in the previous century (radio, television), it can be observes that: technological determinism technological determinism was not the answer, more attempts were to be made to provide answers about the social consequences of television than had ever been asked about radio. In effect, underlying all developments in the media (including the computer) we may assume a basic need for information.

Information became a major concern anywhere during the late 1960 and 1970s where there was simultaneous talk both of 'lack of information' and 'information saturation'. Nowadays, we regard information as a commodity. Train schedules, movies, roadmaps, touristic information, stock prices, we expect it all to be there, preferably online, at no cost. No information, no life. Information drives the economy.

## Commercial impact

We are faced with the question what commercial impact multimedia, and in particular digital convergence, may have. Let's look at some news from business and comments from the popular press. Monique van Dusseldorp & Partners operate on the European multimedia market as consultants. They promote, amongst others, the integration of TV and the Web. Their mission helping clients in Europe position themselves for media convergence. Their interests encompass the following types of content:

— content streaming media (audio and video),

— interactive gaming,

— virtual reality and 3D animation,

— interactive TV programming,

— interactive advertising,

— video on-demand,

— webcasting and multimedia

The advent of broadband Internet access, which has been available in the US for some time but is only now beginning to make inroads into Europe, makes a whole range of new services possible. As download speeds have increased and more bandwidth has become available, the possibility of delivering screen-based content such as films, television programs and music has moved a step closer to mass market usage.

Gaining competitive advantage and future revenue in Europe's broadband landscape will depend heavily on a company's ability to offer integrated services: access (fixed and wireless) and content. It is virtually impossible at this point for one single company to offer these services on a pan-European level. This means that companies need to find partners to fill the gaps in their offerings.

Large investments are being made (by both cable and telephone companies) to improve the technological infrastructure for the new media. The wireless web is being unleashed. Cellular providers around the globe are spending billions of dollars to bring faster connectivity to cell phones, personal digital assistants (PDAs) and other mobile devices. As new networks roll out, wirelessly streamed music will be a huge hit with commuters, while young media junkies will demand music videos and short animations. Tens of millions of consumers around the world will use wireless devices to gain ubiquitous access to content.

The arrival of the Internet has significantly affected how companies approach their strategic priorities across most modern, information-dependent industries. With regard to the media and entertainment industries, this global technological development has transformed information delivery in such a fashion that internal efficiency, customer retention, external competition and the nature of their core product offerings constantly need strategic re-evaluation.

As products become more readily available to consumers through mediums and technologies that utilize the Internet through high speeds, traditional media firms have felt the need to make drastic adaptations in strategy to harness such technologies. The alternative is to be left behind. Statistics on the use of the Internet are compelling.

In the U.S., one in four consumer households connects to the Internet using some sort of highspeed (or "broadband") access, with the use of cable modem connections constituting half of this figure.The implications of this figure for media content over the Internet, or "multimedia", are also noteworthy.

According to McKinsey Consulting, as broadband Internet penetration has increased, so too has the use of entertainment and media products via the Internet. In Europe, the forecasted growth of Internet use through various regions and diversity of broadband mediums is also significant. In adapting and responding to such changes, traditional media firms have undergone various business combinations with non-traditional industry entrants from the telecommunications and Internet industries.

The size of the deals, be they mergers or alliances, have often proven to be large. The business strategies, motives and visions behind the deals have also been significant, as the proponents of the combinations claim to a stake in the imminent convergence of various industries. An empirical oversight and consideration of such business trends is warranted to determine where these deals originate from and what they harvest for the companies involved.

From a strategic management perspective, recent growth activities and business combination trends amongst selected media, cable, telecommunications and Internet firms with regard to the convergence of communications mediums, content and functions. A significant portion of future media content distribution will be determined by developments in various forms of broadband communications access.

Additionally, the impact of pivotal regulatory changes brought about through changes in technology and consumer demand will be covered. Vertical integration developments will be covered from the mid 1980s for some firms, to the present day "digital" data transference standards of high-bandwidth communications.

In the current, dynamic age of the Information Economy, there exist many forces that drive the consolidation of information mediums for the benefits of convenience and simplicity for consumers. Over the past decade, companies providing previously autonomous forms of communications and media products have raced to combine their tangible and intangible assets in order to capitalize on the evolving technological and business trends that were transforming their industries.

Such products and services as terrestrial and cable television, voice telephony, music and filmed entertainment, radio, and more recently, data computing and Internet services are increasingly envisioned as being offered not through separate appliances and channels, but through progressive hardware that unifies all creative and distribution platforms.

Subsequently the businesses that developed these freestanding products are partnering, merging, acquiring or being acquired to allow for increased scale and expertise in the hyper-competitive information marketplace. The term used to define and qualify these trends is "convergence", and its descriptive applications can thus be broadened beyond the technical and theoretical to review the actual business combinations themselves.

To understand these business trends amongst the telecommunications, media and Internet industries, one must grasp the technical meaning and significance of convergence as it applies to communications services. One must also consider the theoretical applications of "vertical integration" as it applies to corporate strategy and how it has related to media convergence over the past decade of inter-industry activity.

With the advent of the Internet and its all-encompassing accommodation of content transmission data transference into digital "bits", the technical implication of information convergence involves the ability of one conduit or channel to carry previously divergent "network platforms" to consumers.

Thus, for instance, fiber optic broadband cables will transmit voice telephony, data Internet text (emails, images, documents), music, video or a combination of them simultaneously. Alternatively, these many different technologies or platforms, due to the "digitization" of data, can also co-exist while evolving in their own right. In other words, mobile phones will download CD-quality music, digital television sets will offer interactive communication over the Internet with vendors, and personal computers can inversely become non-interactive entertainment devices that can simply download a feature film or music video.

Weighing the significance of evolving digital technology in further detail, one sees the impetus behind information convergence. Binary digital language (messages comprised rudimentarily as "0s" and "1s") transmission has proven better and far more efficient than decades-old, wave-based analogue data transmission.

"Digital", then, presents better clarity of information and images due to data transfers that lack inefficient redundancy features inherent with the analogue format. Digital also allows for an increased data carriage capacity, which translates into an exponential increase of voice and visual information offered over scalable conduits such as broadband cable or low-orbit satellite transmissions.

Such data becomes scalable as compressed-form frequencies over fiber optic "pipes", which presents opportunities for providing greater and more sophisticated communications services to a large customer base. In an intuitive business sense, digital media convergence involves the increasing tendency of the previously separate worlds of broadcasting, film, telephony, cable and satellite television, publishing and personal computing to become involved in each other's businesses.

As the technologies evolve to theoretically benefit consumers, the companies who practice control over those technologies, mediums and content will stand to benefit greatly. Visionary CEOs of such companies who have sensed the arrival of convergence have attempted to become gatekeepers to the information channels and content. In order to achieve such goals, the standard corporate practice has involved amassing related communications assets into one company's production and distribution hierarchy, or "vertical integration".

According to economists Scherer and Ross, "vertical integration in the static sense describes the extent to which firms cover the entire spectrum of production and distribution stages. "Motives for vertical integration include reducing the costs of production and giving a producer enhanced control over their economic environment. The two kinds of vertical integration are upstream and downstream integration.

Upstream, or backward vertical integration, involves the owning and producing of the raw materials that might otherwise arrive from independent, external producers. A firm would thus integrate upstream in order to ensure that the supply of its raw materials is available in "shortages and price squeezes by monopolistic suppliers."

Downstream, or forward vertical integration, involves controlling the final or finishing steps of "semi-fabricated products and the wholesaling and retailing operations that deliver goods to consumers. "In the context of the evolving media content and distribution industries, upstream integration involves a content distribution firm (TV network, cable or pure Internet firm) buying a content producer, whereas downstream integration is analogous to primarily content producing firms acquiring distribution channels for transmitting their in-house generated programming (this content here qualifies as the "raw materials and product fabrication" of the media industry).

Overall, owning the production and multiple distribution means of transmitting said content to consumers underscores vertical integration in the digital media realm. Ultimately, vertical integration of separate communications assets and functions within firms is an organizational and evolutionary precursor to the notion of a fully convergent media horizon, where both information bits and their conduits become unified in form and delivery.

In a sense, convergence through vertical integration has been both a result and response to changing technologies and regulations within the telecommunications and media industries. According to author Bruce Wasserstein, "technology has created industries like wireless telephony and satellite TV, and promises a convergence of voice, video and data transmission that will dissolve the boundaries between participants."

Advances in wireless telephony, Internet and broadband cable infrastructure forced regulators to acknowledge that if the traditional phone companies did not adjust their strategic capabilities in an increasingly competitive international sector, they would perish. Said firms acted aggressively in response to easing regulations by diversifying their technical service offerings in efforts to vertically integrate functions through acquisitions.

The main corporate strategies for combining divergent media assets over the past ten to fifteen years have been mergers and acquisitions (M&As). Amongst the various types of M&As outlined by Joseph Bower of Harvard University, many large, recent deals occurring between traditional media, telecommunications, cable systems and Internet companies qualify as "Industry Convergence M&As. "Such deals entail "...inventing an industry and a business model based on an unproven hypothesis: That major synergies can be achieved by culling resources from existing industries whose boundaries seem to be disappearing."

These qualities resemble the stated goals of many industry executives who often rely more on vision rather than empirical support for their merger actions. Bower continues to state that "...attempts to gain strategic leverage by assembling disparate companies are idiosyncratic," and that despite the involvement of conglomerates, such M&As are really entrepreneurial "[activities] in progress."

Despite M&A authority Bruce Wasserstein's assertion that many telecom and media CEOs seek the development of "sound and executable" corporate strategies at justifiable prices, he resonates Bower's view by revealing that many such M&A and even alliance decisions follow the conventional industry wisdom of the moment. The implications behind such managerial motivations are obviously critical for the future of such firms, their shareholders and customers.

Whether firms need to rely on M&A activity to meet the technological, regulatory and economic challenges facing their industries lies at the center of the issue of media convergence. Other forms of corporate strategic integration that have helped pave the way for convergence include horizontal mergers, related business entry and "pure conglomerate" industry entries.

Like vertical integration trends within the media and communications industries, these methods are also brought about increasingly through M&As. A strategic horizontal integration can thus involve acquiring a firm with the same or related business as the acquirer, or one with a related, but not quite the same, business model. The firm can also commit a "pure conglomerate" acquisition, where it laterally enters a completely different business or industry.

In short, there are various interrelated forms of convergence occurring within the media, communications and Internet industries. Industry, corporate, technological, channel and end product (in this case, media content) convergences are occurring on behalf of the interests of visionary managers, company shareholders and ideally the consumers. An in-depth look at the deal events, strategies and external factors to some of these deals will help determine whether any strategic trends have taken place to back the visions of such corporations.

## Digital Convergence in the Media Sector

In the drive towards information convergence, unique content serves as a vital factor in the vertical integration of products with distribution resources. The Internet has shown that information products previously distributed through distinct mediums can be offered uniquely over one medium with its evolving distribution tools.

Content and information such as printed and broadcast-news, educational resources and entertainment have traditionally been offered through publishing, media and entertainment companies. Amongst these companies, vertical integration practices predated the Internet, yet have accelerated with this medium's arrival.

Movie studios buying theatre chains, cable television companies investing heavily in content networks and publishing firms consolidating content library assets by acquiring music labels represent some earlier attempts at vertical integration. Larger deals where whole media conglomerates merged have occurred more recently over the 1990s and into the millennium.

Such firms also engage in strategic alliances to share their content on new distribution platforms - thus testing said platforms for long-term business viability without committing to the wholesale investments that M&As inherently require. The motivations for utilizing either M&As for vertical integration or partnerships include adjusting corporate and business strategies to remain competitive amidst changing regulatory and technological trends and achieving scale in current businesses.

They also include attempts at locking in a customer base where mere loyalty to uniquely produced content may not be enough to prevent substitutability and subsequent customer exit. In other words, when switching costs have been lowered due to the entry of compelling content from a competitor, a media firm will seek to protect its business through a business combination involving another content or content distribution firm.

The envisioned result of a combination would be to offer unique products or services or enforce cost features to lock in customers and even erect barriers to entry by rival media firms. Australian-based News Corporation, Ltd. (News) was amongst the earliest movers in the modern media vertical integration game. In 1985, CEO Rupert Murdoch sought to expand News' reach and reputation globally by acquiring the Twentieth Century Fox film and television studios (Fox) for a total of US$575 million. This move secured valuable extended content and distribution links for the print media giant.

Murdoch recognized that Fox represented a premiere brand in entertainment content that would generate global viewership demand. On one hand, the acquisition illustrated an upstream vertical integration where a print media distributor bought content to generate further entertainment product for its publishing arm to promote.

Yet this was really a combination of strategies because News also performed a product extension by increasing its media asset range to include film and television. With the subsequent purchases of six American television broadcast stations from Metromedia for $1.65 billion and fourteen magazines from the Ziff-Davis publishing company in 1985, News tripled its asset base to $5.6 billion.

Such acquisitions implemented cross-border strategies and market extensions to attain further channels for distributing News' increasingly diversified content. In this way, the publishing buy represented a horizontal merger of print and publishing brands and a market penetration into core media properties.

News increased its strategic assets by upgrading its market reputation, advertising platforms and market knowledge base. Murdoch's goal of establishing a fourth American television broadcast network with News' Fox Broadcasting Company (FBC) necessitated the risky purchases of such television assets.

In 1986, a seventh television station purchase for $28 million in Boston extended FBC's national reach to 25%. The purchase of New World Communications from billionaire Ron Perelman for $2.7 billion later gave FBC assets to expand its owned TV station groups to reach 40% of the U.S. viewing public. Initial acquisitions by debt quadrupled News' liabilities to $2.5 billion from 1984 to 1986.

Yet improving divisional revenue figures and disposal assets provided reassurance for analysts and investors that legitimate growth was underway and that News' long-term integration strategy was working. With

FBC, News performed a gradual downstream vertical integration by establishing a key expanded television distribution network.

In UK, news' prior strategic motives have involved growth of the firm into ancillary media markets. Yet News' most recent competitive advantage in the media business has been satellite television transmission. With its evolving satellite strategies, News seeks to capitalize on a unique form of digital convergence in media that will rival broadband cable technologies. Commercial satellites presented cost efficiency and scale benefits over terrestrial and cable television, which required large investments in infrastructure to establish landlines, switches, receivers and other hardware necessary for television signal transmission.

By contrast, satellite transmission initially required renting relay devices on communications satellites ("transponders") at a fraction of the cost of setting up other hardware. With satellites, independent TV stations and cable networks could secure national distribution for transmission that was competitive with more established broadcast networks. Sensing such technical, cost and strategic advantages, News invested in satellites in the UK in 1983 and established a first to market position, a foundation that allowed for easier regional growth in Europe.

Merging with a larger satellite consortium and locking in premium programming through subscription-based rather than advertising-based business plans, News' British Sky Broadcasting plc (BSkyB) came to dominate the broadcast satellite field in the UK. Some key strategic assets BSkyB sealed included becoming a natural monopoly, erecting barriers to entry and establishing exclusive licensing to distribute content with the leading Hollywood studios.

Until 1997, BSkyB remained the sole satellite provider in the UK, which provided negotiating power for premium content. Thus, BSkyB reduced the power of its suppliers and its buyers, considering that the threat of substitutes in the region were low. With improved technical features for tracking subscriber data and customized pay-per-view options, BSkyB locked in customers, built scaled growth and harnessed a competitive edge by positioning itself for the introduction of digital TV.

The television "set-top boxes" that enabled any sort of digital television reception for consumers were under the control of BSkyB's subsidiary. By acquiring Digi-Media Vision, a video technology firm, and forming an alliance named British Interactive Broadcasting (BIB) in 1997, BSkyB tried to tackle interactive satellite TV.

The company continues to harness innovation in media convergence. In July 2001, it unveiled a "next generation" digital set-top box called "Sky+" which integrates a satellite receiver and video recorder so that consumers can record one program while viewing another.

Rupert Murdoch's next strategic vision involves linking distinct satellite assets based in different continents to offer News' programming to as wide a global audience base as possible. By bidding aggressively for DirecTV, North America's biggest satellite operator, he is drawing closer to that goal. News' total satellite operations worldwide are linked under an umbrella organization labeled Sky Global Networks (SGN).

Adding DirecTV would give SGN an additional 10 million pay TV consumers from the leading media market in the world, bringing its global residential satellite reach to approximately 95 million. In America alone, SGN's subscription base would draw close to AOL Time Warner's numbers of 13 million. The deal has been pending for some time, and if it is finalized, News would own 30% of the combined DirecTV-SGN, with current parent Hughes Electronics' shareholders and other investors holding the rest.

Yet News would gain operational control of the firm. The acquisition would strategically represent a horizontal merger and market extension into annexing further assets into an already strong satellite empire. Considering News' current advertising-based broadcasting platform in the U.S., DirecTV's purchase would diversify away from News' subscription-based U.S. holdings to provide a valuable content exclusivity scheme in America.

Attaining DirecTV would also pose a competitive threat to American cable providers, who sense that SGN's huge scale and customer reach in America would give it substantial leverage over programming and carriage fees. With a war chest of news, sports and entertainment offerings, News' divisions are on par with those of rival cable programmers.

Yet interestingly, the U.S. Cable Act of 1992, a key regulatory hurdle against programming exclusivity for vertically integrated cable firms like AOL Time Warner, does not apply to satellite broadcasters. With this strategic barrier lowered, News could impose exclusivity on its program offerings in the U.S. as it had done earlier in the U.K. with BSkyB.

Additionally, News has an ownership stake in the leading interactive TV channel-guide service Gemstar-TV Guide, a property that would present technical synergies with DirecTV's integrated personal video recording capabilities. A satellite subscriber would be presented with advanced interactive, digital and program storage functionalities while News could track transaction revenues from its subscriber base.

These features would threaten to take subscribers away and lock them in from cable firms unless and until comparable broadband features countered them. All of these factors would give News formidable competitive tools to take on its cable rivals. The only seemingly missing piece of News' strategy is a strong, central Internet brand to accompany its distribution outlets.

Arguably one of the largest entertainment firms in the world with a distinctly ubiquitous brand name, The Walt Disney Company (Disney) has established itself as a premier generator of original entertainment content. Although a diversified entertainment firm with various asset holdings , Disney's core competencies involve drawing upon new and classic entertainment brands through its film studios and libraries and exploiting them through ancillary assets.

Thus a hit movie or TV show can become a featured attraction at a Disney theme park. An aggressive competitor in the traditional media market, Disney's future intentions involve extending its brands into evolving new media channels. Yet before reaching that level of distribution, Disney must determine its strategic priorities regarding business combinations with key digital players to help it access such channels.

Disney's limited yet significant M&A history provide indications of how the firm has strategically adjusted to major industry changes. In 1971, the U.S. Justice Department and Federal Communications Commission (FCC) issued a consent decree barring TV and feature film producers from owning their respective distribution outlets, and TV networks from owning content production and syndication assets.

The decree, known as the Financial Interest and Syndication (Fin-Syn) rules, aimed to prevent the formation of integrated media monopolies. Yet Fin-Syn and the FCC were becoming more relaxed in the mid to late 1980s, as indicated by News' establishing of the Fox Broadcasting Company alongside Fox Studios.

In 1987, partly as a competitive response to the Fox development, and partly as a strategic move into content distribution, Disney commenced a downstream vertical integration strategy into broadcast television by acquiring Los Angeles' largest independent television station for $323 million. This acquisition created a "donor-recipient mode" of value creation, where Disney successfully provided a programming and financial performance upgrade to the station.

By the early 1990s, TV networks felt that they were constrained by Fin-Syn in a media climate where content programmers' clout was increasing. Deregulation followed with the repeal of Fin-Syn allowing networks to produce and own 100% equity in the programs they aired, rather than buy them exclusively from traditional studio suppliers. TV networks thus integrated upstream to secure their own content supplies and establish product-specific economies of scale.

In turn, feeling threatened by a potential drought of network activity, some of the large content "sellers", or studios, either launched their own or acquired top-tier broadcast networks to secure their television distribution channels. Disney was the first to perform the latter act in the post Fin-Syn era. Despite its rise to financial strength and market leadership in the 1990s, Disney was not known for implementing acquisitions as a significant corporate strategy.

The firm had primarily grown and gained media market share through implementing strategies such as leveraging internal content resources into expanding media channels (e.g. home video and cable television) and new markets such as consumer products. In 1995, Disney acquired Capital Cities/American Broadcasting Company (ABC), then the leading American television network for $19 billion in cash and stock.

The underlying motive was to vertically integrate forward by adding a critical television distribution outlet for Disney Studios while performing horizontal integration by collecting ABC's original content assets (journalistic, sports and original dramatic programming) into its own asset pool. With ABC came multiple television and radio stations in leading American media markets and a major sports-cable network.

Having proven that it could manage a television station, Disney now expanded its scale and broadcast market penetration with a network buy that brought about a "collusive mode" of value creation. The strategic assets of brand, content and scaled reach were pooled from both Disney and ABC for a sustainable competitive advantage over rivals Viacom, Time Warner, Seagram Universal and News' Fox divisions.

Although with the acquisition Disney removed an imminent content competitor in broadcasting in order to extend its own content and distribution assets, ABC was not and is not solely dependent on Disney's content for broadcast television. Thus ABC was only "partially integrated" so as to meet industry competitive standards. With a recent strategic buy aimed at producing market penetration and product extension, Disney announced its purchase of Fox Family Worldwide from News Corporation and Saban Entertainment for $3.3 billion in cash, plus the assumption of $2 billion in debt.

The cable TV properties inherent with the purchase drive Disney's programming further to 81 million cable and satellite TV subscribers in the U.S., annex new content products into its already existing markets, and deepen Disney's presence in European and Latin American markets which it is already in. Disney should expect a high level of symbiosis in integrating Fox Family's content, considering that the latter's slate of family-oriented programming complements Disney's similar core competency perfectly.

Finally, in light of the mid-2001 economic slowdown in the U.S., this deal creates a deal strategy consisting of a new advertising platform to assist Disney's cash flow at the cable network level, while also mining additional TV affiliate fees to offset any further potential advertising downturns.

The past deals have further strengthened the Disney brand across its multiple platforms, yet its foray into the Internet has proven difficult. Disney's large scale entry into the online arena commenced in 1998 with a 43% equity investment in Internet search 30 engine Infoseek, which lead to a full acquisition a year later.

Currently, Disney's online strategy involves promotions and direct marketing with various websites bearing the names of Disney's offline cable and broadcast TV properties like ESPN.com and ABCNEWS.com. The combined unit, known as Walt Disney Internet Group, is involved in licensing partnerships with various wireless companies, Internet firms and advertisers. Disney's distribution status with the Internet presents the main weakness in its strategy towards digital convergence.

The company, although having a diversified Internet presence and stellar, global content properties, does not retain a "gatekeeper" status with regard to any platform that allows for digital content transmission. Threats include competitors such as News and AOL Time Warner, two firms that could secure negotiating advantages over Disney's products through the cable and satellite ends of the media distribution value chain should Disney not secure its own integrated broadband conduit.

Disney's strategic assets include those of reputation, premium content, advertising leverage and market knowledge. Yet it harbours ambitions to distribute movies over the Internet through the use of video-on-demand technologies and wireless set-top boxes.

A formidable media competitor to News and Disney, Viacom too acquired content and distribution assets in order to vertically integrate them, adapt and grow as a firm. Viacom achieved its position as a top four media company by aggregating cable television networks, TV and film production, video distribution and publishing firms under one roof.

A media product's life and brand, be it a feature film, television program or book, could then pass through the various segments of the company in order to generate revenue. The company was founded in 1971 when top three broadcast network CBS spun off its entertainment programming production and syndication divisions in response to the U.S. Justice Department's Fin-Syn consent decree.

Throughout the 1970s and 80s, the firm acquired TV, radio and cable TV stations to integrate forward into distribution. Sensing growth in cable programming, Viacom launched "pay cable" movie network Showtime in 1976 and acquired MTV Networks and Nickelodeon in 1985, two "basic cable" networks that featured music videos and children's animation, respectively.

One of the more active recent entrants into the global media space has been Vivendi Universal (Vivendi) of France. The company had sustained closely with the French government as a water utility, real estate and construction, communications and environmental firm prior to the arrival of CEO Jean-Marie Messier in 1996.

Many of Vivendi's diversified businesses were necessities for French and European consumers and thus maintained prolonged maturity phases in their respective product life cycles. Vivendi's 49% investment in Canal Plus, continental Europe's largest pay-TV firm, as well as partnerships in European telecommunications concerns, gave Messier a vision of expanding Vivendi into a media and communications company in order to capture the growth of converging information businesses.

Managerial hubris was presumably another motivation, as Messier watched the AOL Time Warner merger and Rupert Murdoch's global media consolidations utilize resources he felt Vivendi also retained and could leverage successfully. Thus in June 2000, Vivendi commenced merger discussions with Canal Plus and Canada's Seagram, the latter owning Universal Studios and Music Group in Hollywood.

The entailed strategy involved combining the Universal and Canal Plus film libraries (a combined catalogue of over 9,000 content properties), the largest music company in the world, an expanding theme park business, Canal Plus' European pay-TV platform, and Vivendi's telephony and Internet interests in a vertically integrated organization rivaling the other large media firms.

For Universal Studios, this merger proposal further validated the value of media content in the age of consolidation and convergence. Vivendi, like Seagram and Matsushita before it, performed a pure conglomerate merger by acquiring its content assets. Although retaining investment interests in cable television and wireless telephony, Vivendi's core competencies were spread over multiple non-media activities.

Vivendi's diversification into media resulted in a confirmed share for share merger between the three firms in 2001 valued at US$34 billion. For Seagram, the merger provided digital conduits, added financial strength and film market penetration for scale in competing with long-standing rivals Time Warner, Paramount and Twentieth Century Fox. This deal illustrated the "participative mode" of value creation, where the pooling of the combining firms' resources allow for synergies, scale and scope economies.

The deal also confirmed the fact that M&As are the fastest means for entering a market , and "time to market" has proven critical in the fast-paced media and telecommunications convergence environment. Although the Vivendi-Seagram-Canal Plus merger sought to gain competitive advantages in the media product market, one merger motive it did not seek nor achieve was risk reduction.

The parties agreed to divest Seagram's spirits business, a "cash cow" and mature business , and Vivendi's construction business. To secure approval from the European Commission for the merger, Mr. Messier agreed to sell Vivendi's 22.7% stake in BSkyB and avoid anticompetitive practices that the Canal Plus combination would have posed. Vivendi has yet to successfully accomplish this.

Vivendi's share price dropped 40% due to investor fears over the French utility stalwart's massive entry into multiple 'speculative' businesses as well as the divestiture of its stable businesses [please see Exhibit 3.9 for a returns index profile of the company's local financial performance]. Unlike News/BSkyB and AOL Time Warner yet similar to Disney and Viacom, Vivendi's "gatekeeper" power over its evolving digital content is primarily Internet based.

Vivendi does not own a satellite or cable infrastructure; it claims wireless telephony as its main proprietary digital platform. Yet the Internet is a free domain, and customers could choose alternative portals to Vizzavi, which is Vivendi's wireless portal formed through a 50/50 partnership with Vodafone. Additionally, the European Commission banished Vivendi's chances for content exclusivity by requiring availability of Universal's content to rivals "on fair terms."

Lastly, the uncertain state of consumer demand over multiple digital platform offerings may ultimately affect

Vivendi's attempts to integrate its communications divisions while building value. Vivendi's assets in its general and digital content strategy include local market knowledge and technical flexibility with its evolving multiple distribution platforms.

These platforms include wireless, cable TV network and general Internet access, although the latter has been criticized as lacking any barriers to entry and faces many substitutes. The firm has also deployed focused business combination strategies to capitalize on its core competences. On the back of positive recent revenue figures driven by its television, telecom and film units , Vivendi has continued acquiring to supplement its content and distribution channels for digital convergence.

To leverage its massive music assets online, it acquired U.S.-based online music distribution service MP3.com for $372 million. Although also utilizing partnerships with other content, technology and distribution firms, Vivendi chose to acquire MP3.com because its disruptive technology was ubiquitous on the Internet. The move removed a potential competitor of Vivendi's in the digital end of the music distribution value chain, a classic defensive use of M&A strategy.

As it has done with most of its acquisitions in the media and Internet industries, Vivendi has chosen a "preservation" integration process with MP3.com while it facilitates synergies with MP3.com's core competencies. Vivendi will allow this technology firm to design legal online music distribution tools that will utilize Universal Music's content, and has not altered the acquired firm's management or significant internal processes post-acquisition.

The firm counts this "hands-off" approach as entrepreneurial and a cultural strength in light of its cross-Atlantic entry status into the American media market. This strength is pushed through industry alliances Vivendi has utilized in the content and distribution sectors. By partnering with Sony Music to launch Pressplay.com, an online music distribution and subscription service, Vivendi allows MP3.com to build the technical infrastructure for the joint service.

Through the alliance with Sony, Vivendi retains a key benefit of business alliances: Access to complementary assets (in this case, Sony's global music catalogue and library) without the investment risks of acquiring such assets. Other strategic strengths include its European-based presence, and emphasis on local entertainment for diversified consumer appeal.

The company emphasizes the marketing of music to local tastes in America, Europe and other territories by retaining diverse artists on its labels. As Universal Music is "omnipresent", so has been the company's general long-term strategic emphasis with regard to content. Vivendi has used M&As in the media, communications and Internet sectors to achieve fast market entry while partnering to test digital content distribution.

## Convergence in Cable and Telecommunications Sectors

In the mid 1990s, key deregulatory changes in the United States allowed for cross-sector mergers and consolidations within the communications industry. In a much more competitive domain, some of these consolidations produced companies that took advantage of technological advancements within telecommunications in order to offer multiple, convergent services (often referred to as "bundled" telecom services).

The U.S. Telecommunications Act of 1996 allowed television networks to own cable TV systems, authorized competitive local exchange carrier telephone companies (CLECs) to enter long distance telephony and allowed cross-entry between telephone companies and cable industry carriers. Additionally, larger long distance carriers were enabled to offer local telephone services.

CLECs offering advanced local fiber optic network technology were able to provide voice telephony, data, video and Internet transmission services directly to business customers while bypassing the incumbent's locally wired loops and connect directly to long distance carriers. The Act thus increased competition by significantly lowering traditional barriers to entry into the telecommunications industry.

The smaller telecom competitors who entered the market eventually took part in widespread consolidations to build competitive scale against larger incumbents such as AT&T, GTE and MCI. The business combinations resulting from this environment helped form companies with technologies capable of providing, in theory, additional broadband conduits for the transmission of high-bandwidth media content.

One of the fastest growing CLECs in the U.S. was WorldCom, Inc. (WorldCom), a firm that built scale and bundled services primarily through M&As. In an ambitious move that proved definitive of the post deregulatory consolidation deals within the telecommunications industry, WorldCom acquired MCI Communications Corp. (MCI) for $43.4 billion in 1998.

Through the acquisition, WorldCom sought the speed of positioning itself as a premier, fully integrated communications company that offered extended local, long distance, Internet and wireless services. Although already offering many of these services globally, WorldCom captured significant growth through the benefits of scale offered by MCI's synergetic assets.

The move thus represented a significant market penetration for WorldCom, where MCI's long distance telecom service (itself built up through MCI's own acquisitions and representing 90% of MCI's operating income ) and Internet services increased the combined company's customer reach and product scope. The subsequent scale of the firm provided a strong, integrated national base for advanced Internet and data services via Digital Subscriber (DSL).

As of the end of 2000, MCI/WorldCom claimed to have the largest Internet backbone infrastructure in the U.S., which expectedly set a firm foundation for the future transmission of developing media content via DSL conduits. Yet MCI/WorldCom has recently encountered slower margin growth and expansion difficulties affecting its share price.

Despite past growth through M&As with CLECs and digital infrastructure players , WorldCom reached an impasse when its ambitious bid to merge with long distance and wireless U.S. telephone giant Sprint was broken up in the second quarter of 2000. The Sprint issue, as well as the absence of a wireless telephony strategy, have affected investor confidence in the firm.

The Nasdaq listed stock price dropped from a 52-week high of $49/share to $14.28/share by early July

2001. So, in June 2001 the company decided to split its businesses into two publicly traded tracking stocks:

1) WorldCom Group, which will pursue growth businesses such as broadband, wireless and IP services, and

2) MCI Group, which will focus on the "cash cow", or cash flow generating long distance telephony business (estimated at comprising 40% of overall revenues through 2001). The latter division will be exposed to extreme competitive pressures in the next few years. This new strategy of focusing on web hosting and high-end IP services is expected to revive the company's favour with investors.

With deregulation, the Internet's increasing adoption by the public and the rate of technological change encouraging competition in the telecommunications and cable industries, deals like MCI/WorldCom only encouraged similar or bigger mergers aimed at capturing competitive advantages. Additionally, the product life cycle of communications products shifted in the mid-1990s, with long distance voice telephony becoming increasingly categorized as a commodity business.

Standard voice over copper wiring was considered in a long maturity phase of the communications product life cycle when compared to the growing potential for voice over Internet protocol (VOIP) and video transference. In considering their resource-based strategy options during this time of rapid technological change, many telecom firms therefore chose adaptability to new information resources tied to the Internet over the continuity of focusing on their commodified businesses.

In the midst of increasing competition, the oldest and largest U.S. telecom firm too felt the pressure to adapt quickly to this period of innovation. AT&T Corporation (AT&T) adopted aggressive corporate and business strategies in the cable arena to transform itself from a long distance voice provider to a full service, integrated communications company. With a series of M&As, AT&T executed on its motives of:

— upgrading corporate resources to deliver high speed Internet services;

— securing the speed of positioning itself as a broadband telecommunications leader amidst competition from MCI/WorldCom and GTE;

— attaining complementary assets by entering the residential telephone business and absorbing cable properties into its standard telephony activities to do so;

— achieving significant firm growth through amassing well performing and progressive assets; and

— finding competitive advantages in its existing voice product markets.

With such an all-encompassing vision, AT&T hoped to be the premiere platform for traditional communications as well as for the future of new media transmission - a vertically integrated vehicle for digital convergence. AT&T's massive shift in strategy and subsequent status serve as the quintessential case study of the effects of M&As on a large company within the digital convergence arena as well as of the current state of convergence via broadband cable.

Acquiring Teleport Communications for $11 billion then gave AT&T local business customer access via fiber optic cable, thus bypassing the regional phone competitors who previously charged AT&T fees for such access. These purchases represented critical product extensions into the Internet arena and AT&T integrated the two firms by bundling local phone services and features with its consumer long distance offerings.

Considering the related nature of said firms' communications services the buys also represented horizontal mergers for AT&T in broadening its core communications competencies. While the above represented entry for AT&T into advanced Internet services, the following mergers represented building scale through securing the conduit best believed to inevitably carry high-speed digital voice and data services - cable.

The $69.8 billion 1998 conglomerate merger with Tele-Communications International Inc. (TCI) and $62 billion follow-up acquisition of MediaOne Group in 1999 illustrated AT&T's bet on evolving cable technologies as the future of wireline communications. Higher capacity fiber optic cable that could carry two-way video, voice, data and interactive content was replacing the traditional downstream coaxial cables that the industry had relied upon for decades, thus opening up the possibilities for digital convergence.

Initially, a joint venture between AT&T and TCI was envisioned, yet structural difficulties forced both sides to discuss a full merger of its cable operations with AT&T. For the vision of seamless access to work, a merger and downstream vertical integration of the complete cable infrastructure was necessary. With TCI came Liberty Media Group, a cable programming arm that would become a distinct division of AT&T run by TCI's CEO John Malone.

By removing significant barriers to entry and providing access to distribution channels, the deregulations of 1996 allowed for the smaller yet highly competitive regional Bell operating companies to enter long distance telephony and threaten AT&T's. core competency. By merging cable with telephony through its acquisitions, AT&T sought first-to-market status as a large, cable-based broadband provider, and in effect, shifted its core competency away from pure long distance services towards cable and local telephony through cable.

Fully integrated communications services therefore constituted product differentiation through wholly new distribution channels, causing inimitability for traditional telecommunications and cable firms. Initially, AT&T's vision of building a convergent medium for all customer communication needs was well received.

It's stock rose from $31/share at the TCI acquisition announcement to $48/share at the MediaOne deal confirmation. Yet the firm has had difficulties bringing that vision to reality, due to both internal and external factors. Although AT&T bet on broadband as the future of telecommunications, it failed to upgrade and integrate its cable assets quickly enough for a strong rollout of such services to customers. AT&T misjudged how long the cable integration and broadband service rollout would take against the need to raise its margins and pay down debt.

Additionally, its core long distance telephony business started to deteriorate (due to competition and an internal de-emphasis vis-a-vis the shift in focus towards broadband) before a new revenue sources could be established. AT&T's stock fell after its announcement on 2 May 2000 that it would miss its sales targets.

Meanwhile, high fixed costs remained from the cable acquisitions. Close to $40 billion was spent in capital upgrades of cable properties to accommodate Internet and phone traffic, and shareholders became distressed that the firm wasn't executing fast enough on its convergent strategies.

To appease them, Armstrong announced in October 2000 that AT&T would be split into four separately run, publicly traded firms: Wireless, consumer long distance services, business services and broadband cable. Although the company claimed that non-voice businesses had grown, the weight of AT&T's debt prevented similar cash flow figures, thus prompting such splits to enable said divisions to carry their own currencies and increase shareholder value.

Liberty Media, the programming arm that came with TCI, was also recently spun off into a separately traded company from AT&T. These measures have indicated reversals of the vertical integration strategies that assembled AT&T's properties under one roof. They also imply that different core competencies had clashed at AT&T, where voice telephony still comprises a significant portion of its business amidst all ongoing cable consolidations.

In its striving for competitive advantage at a critical period of channel and business convergence, AT&T may have taken on more than it could effectively manage. According to strategy authors Hamel and Prahalad, core competencies:

1. Make a disproportionate contribution to ultimate customer value, or to the efficiency with which that value is delivered, and
2. Provide a basis for entering new markets.

AT&T's management would claim that its past competencies in voice telecommunications and servicing of a wide continental customer base, coupled with the effects of technological changes and deregulations, justify its shift into broader competencies involving local phone, cable and Internet services. Management would embrace the core competency theory's presumptions in justifying their product extensions.

AT&T also re-emphasized its belief in offering bundled communications services through broadband cable. Yet by planning to separate the company into four divisions, AT&T has admitted to needing to manage distinctive competencies accordingly. Overpayment may be due to over-optimism in acquisition assumptions, overestimation of expected synergies, simply overbidding, or poor post-acquisition integration; all of which have been described as applicable to AT&T by critics.

Another insight involves the likelihood of vertical integration compounding independent risks rather than diffusing them. While AT&T was meeting the risks inherent with cable's costly technical upgrades, the risks of the long distance segment's maturity and declining margins hurt the rest of its business. Tellingly, both AT&T and MCI/WorldCom have chosen to split the management of their businesses along growth, maturity and functional parameters to manage their risks separately.

For such reasons, as well as the fact that its cable assets are the largest in North America, rival bidders will challenge AT&T until it shows performance enhancements with its cable platform both financially and functionally. Past business combinations involving cable and Internet companies serve as valuable indicators of the strategic motives and results of convergence-driven deals.

In May 1999, U.S. high-speed Internet access provider At Home Network acquired large Internet portal Excite, Inc. for $7.2 billion in stock. The deal capitalized on the strategies of combining prime Internet content with fast broadband Internet access, and of capturing the latest interactive advertising solutions for online ad buying corporations.

For @Home, the results of the acquisition represented an Internet product extension under Ansoff's matrix, and an upstream vertical integration to annex a seemingly valuable content arm into a strong Internet distribution company. Separately, the firms had gained scale and momentum prior to their merger. Founded as a joint venture by TCI and leading venture capital firm Kleiner Perkins Caulfield & Byers in 1995, @Home secured partnerships and affiliations with many large cable companies to secure access to over 50% of North American homes.

By allying with leading global cable firms through distribution agreements, @Home secured 1) speed to market and 2) access to complementary and regional cable assets to secure customers domestically and abroad. In its efforts to build content assets, @Home acquired Internet media advertising developer Narrative Communications Corp. for $96 million in February 1999.

With this purchase, the firm specialized in advertising and direct marketing as extended core competencies to its primary cable focus and subsequently attracted more online business affiliations.@Home's competitive advantages included advanced market knowledge as well as technical superiorities over alternative access methods to broadband.

Cable's inherent advantages over DSL technology offered by telecom firms included higher sensitivity for data transmission over longer distances, more data carriage capacity and economical system upgrade costs for bundled and interactive services. Although wireless and satellite broadband access required initial less capital outlay (e.g. lack of wire laying construction costs) than cable, cable allowed for true interactivity at a cost savings to consumers compared to the necessary combination of DSL, wireless and satellite technologies.

@Home thereby presented strategic advantages over its product substitutes in broadband access. Originally founded as a start-up Internet software company in 1993, Excite, Inc. quickly rose to become a leading search engine with multiple distribution agreements, including those with MSN and Netscape. In 1996, Excite had a successful IPO, and acquired and thereby removed competing search engines WebCrawler and Magellan.

The company's revenues rose primarily through Internet advertising and distribution fees. The following year Excite launched a multiple channel format reflecting its diverse content offerings and expanded internationally into Europe and Australia. In January 1998, Excite acquired MatchLogic, Inc., a firm that specialized in directed online advertising services. The acquisition strategy involved capitalizing on the large registered user base that Excite retained for more customer focused advertising, theoretically leveraging Excite's market knowledge for keen positioning in an increasingly advertising-based Internet marketplace.

The Excite @Home combination was then partly an extension of Excite's own strategy of leveraging its 28 million users for directed advertising. Monitoring the online viewing and commerce habits of such a large consumer base would allow for progressive means of marketing to them by new and traditional companies who usually advertised via print, radio or television.

As advertising mediums therefore evolved via the Internet, so did the expectation of client capture by the cable firm. A critical acquisition motive and assumption was that Excite's registered user base would become Excite @Home's broadband cable customers. Another key assumption was that the online advertising market would sustain growth. This model of subscriber revenue growing alongside media/advertising revenue seemed like a promising one, considering that one source 66 could offset any possible losses from the other.

Yet the relationship between paying subscribers of Excite@Home's cable service and Excite's web page viewers who help generate advertising income are not necessarily the same. An increase in the former does not always lead to increased advertising income - a factor which can and has in the past undermined the company's integration strategy behind its merger.

The complex ownership structure behind Excite@Home had also lead to disagreements over its strategy. Although an independently traded company, the firm's multiple cable backers are direct competitors. AT&T inherited a 58% voting stake in @Home from its TCI deal, whereas competitors Comcast, Cox Cable and Cablevision split 30% of the stock and 24% of the voting power at the time of the Excite acquisition. In March 2000, AT&T bought 60 million Excite shares from

Comcast and Cox and reorganized Excite's ownership structure.

In January 2001, AT&T increased its economic stake in Excite@Home to 38% stock and a 79% voting interest. Despite Excite's value as a media and advertising asset that would offset the increasingly commoditized subscription business, AT&T was not in favour of @Home's purchase of Excite, preferring to keep the broadband infrastructure as the firm's core competency.

Dwindling advertising spending across all media businesses in 2001 affected Excite@Home's business adversely and reopened talk of divesting Excite from the company. Lack of full ownership over its cable assets, a limit of diversified non-Internet media content, and adverse market conditions have hurt the firm's stock price and long-term viability.

Additionally, Comcast and Cox Cable decided to end their mutually exclusive carriage relationship with the firm six months earlier than scheduled, compromising key access channels. Despite raising $100 million in June 2001 in a sale of convertible notes and $85 million in additional financing from AT&T in part to offset risks for the holders of those notes, Excite@Home lost over 90% of its share valuation from mid-2000 to mid-2001.

Considering that its stock has traded for less than $1.00 for close to a month, the firm faces being de-listed from the Nasdaq Stock Exchange. This will in turn force it to repay the full value of its bond notes or face bankruptcy, with the likely outcome involving Excite@Home selling its cable and media assets to willing rivals.

An applicable theoretical perspective on what happened to this company involves the resource-based theory of strategy and economic rents. Excite@Home's first to market strategy of combining cable and content initially earned high rents due to its innovative high-speed business model and aggressive customer capture. Yet these rents were ultimately Schumpeterian or entrepreneurial, where the innovator earned rents until its inimitability faded.

AOL Time Warner rose as a formidable competitor and earned Ricardian rents due to the comparative scarcity of its long standing corporate reputation, brand, customer reach and more compelling content. In contrast, Excite@Home's competitive superiority declined as its innovation reached what economist Joseph Schumpeter called diffusion, or competitors successfully imitating the innovation and outperforming the innovator. The firm also lacks cost advantages with its broadband applications.

According to McKinsey Consulting, the cost of high-bandwidth infrastructure retention, maintenance, hosting and application development are much higher for broadband application providers than for their narrowband competitors. Said costs will continue to be high in relation to broadband carriers' residual efficiencies and revenue streams until 2004. As costs rose at Excite@Home, so did its reported subscriber and advertising revenue bases, indicating diseconomies of scale.

The company's major broadband competitors such as AT&T and AOL Time Warner have other revenue sources aside from the Internet that allow them to extend their experience curves with broadband services.

Excite@Home does not retain such businesses, has lost inimitability to strong market entrants, and has had to endure unfavourable cost conditions in a nascent market with low switching costs.

As the broadband communications horizon evolved competitively amongst media, telecommunications and cable firms, the leading ISP and search engine in the U.S. felt the need to develop its distribution and access strategies to battle multiple competitive threats. With over 22 million registered subscribers and over 160 million diversified Internet service users, America Online, Inc. (AOL) retained the leading strategic assets of brand and reputation, consumer scale, advertising strength and market knowledge.

AOL posted strong revenue figures in 1999 and 2000, with 76% of its income derived from its subscriber revenue and the rest from advertising and e-commerce. Yet free-of-charge ISPs such as NetZero.com and Microsoft's MSN were posing threats to the majority of AOL's income source. Additionally, AOL felt the need to access broadband infrastructure in order to leverage its brand name and protect a critically necessary downstream distribution channel for its proprietary web content.

With deals by AT&T and Excite@Home emphasizing the integration of high-speed Internet technologies, content and access, AOL felt another competitive threat in light of a maturing dial-up Internet access business. AOL initially objected to the outcomes of business combinations amongst its competitors. AT&T's ownership stake in Excite@Home gave the latter exclusive access to AT&T's cable pipes until 2002.

### *AOL's Initial Broadband Strategies*

Responding to advances in broadband, AOL had committed to partnerships with varying industry players to gain competitive advantage. In early 1999, AOL sided with DSL technology by announcing alliances with Bell Atlantic and Southwestern Bell, two regional Bell operating companies, to deliver broadband connectivity to its subscribers.

Soon thereafter, AOL also partnered with satellite manufacturer Hughes Electronics and Compaq to deliver its service over a satellite link called DirecPC. Yet these business combinations presented various alliance drawbacks including lack of control, difficulty in integrating knowledge, and questionable long-term viability for AOL.

Increasingly, the successful yet alert ISP considered a strategic move of permanence within highspeed access. On 10 January 2000, AOL and media conglomerate Time Warner, Inc. announced that they would merge to create a company capitalizing on the convergence of content and evolving digital communications mediums. The combination was an all-stock transaction valued initially at $350 billion, making it the largest U.S. corporate merger to date.

AOL ultimately agreed to pay $165 billion, a sum with a 70% premium for the "old economy" assets of one of the oldest and largest diversified media firms in the [72] world. Considering cable's previously stated benefits for broadband communications, and that Time Warner retained the second largest cable asset base in the U.S., AOL certainly confronted the uncertainty over the "open access" issue directly by mimicking AT&T's product extension strategy into cable.

Yet the forecasted level of functional synergies to result from the merger made it unique amidst all M&As in the media and communications sectors. For Time Warner, who already had a limited Internet content presence similar to those in Disney's portfolio mentioned above, this merger presented the most viable way to enter the Internet arena for sustainable growth with a leading Internet brand.

Time Warner did not have a successful Internet strategy prior to the merger, despite its Time publishing unit's past forays into digital media. With AOL, Time Warner captured the technological expertise resources and platform to leverage its media holdings online. With the anticipation of increased content distribution converging over the Internet (music, video television and films on demand, interactive and digital television), the merger presented opportunities for a fast time-to-market strategy in adapting a leading media firm's properties into a more integrated, information-based value chain.

Time Warner effectively sought a complete transformation into a new kind of communications firm by joining AOL. Such a corporate transformation implied that significant synergies would need to arise from the merger. The combined firm forecasted $1 billion in "tactical synergies" resulting from the merger. These synergies were split between revenue enhancement opportunities resulting from cross selling between AOL and Time Warner's cable system, television network and publishing assets, and reduced operating expenses.

Such a vision anticipated a participative mode of value creation from the merger, where a collective pooling of respective resources and competences would result in synergies and economies of scope over the diversified media offerings. A desired result of such synergy for AOL involved lessening its dependency on either subscriptions or advertising and rather having a more dynamic, diversified revenue base that included film, music and television distribution and rights licensing.

Although the current expectations for the company in online revenue are strong, the fact that the firm's risk specific to the volatile Internet advertising sector has become manageable shows that synergies are working to an extent. This factor has proven critical with slowing advertising growth adding to the financial troubles of competitors Yahoo! and Excite@Home.

### *Challenges*

Considering the regulatory objections AOL Time Warner had to clear before merging, it is ironic that AOL protested against AT&T and Excite@Home's exclusive relationship the previous year. With vocal opposition to the initial scope of the merger from Disney, NBC broadcast network and Vivendi Universal, AOL Time Warner faced restrictions in the U.S. and Europe.

The Federal Trade Commission (FTC) in the U.S. required nondiscriminatory access to competing Internet services on its cable pipelines, while the Federal Communications Commission (FCC) mandated the opening of its popular Instant Messaging (IM) service to rivals. The European Union in turn prevented the merger of music company EMI Group plc and Time Warner, helped prevent Bertelsmann and AOL from sharing European Internet interest, ordered Vivendi Universal to pull out of AOL France and required the same rules mandated by the FCC regarding IM and access by independent ISPs.

Since then, AOL Time Warner's internal corporate strategy of integrating cultures, technology, shared goals and cost-cutting measures have encountered difficulties in implementation. The post-merger integration involved reorganization steps resulting in 2,400 redundancies; 725 jobs at AOL and the remainder at various Time Warner divisions. Despite reporting a "restructuring liability" of $965 million during Q1 2001 for post-merger activities, the company has performed well through a tough advertising and technology market.

AOL reported 2 million additional online subscribers (putting total membership over 29 million) in April and total company revenues rose 9% in Q1 2001 year-to-year to $9.1 billion, with EBITDA growing 20% to $2.1 billion. Total subscriptions (magazines, cable, Internet) rose 16% to more than 133 million, with digital cable subscriptions quadrupling over the previous year to 3.3 million.

To help meet its aggressive year-end growth targets of $40 billion in revenues and $11 billion in EBITDA, the company also recently raised the monthly price of its Internet service. Yet the second quarter of 2001 proved more difficult, as the company fell short of meeting its targets, and recently announced another 1000 layoffs.

In short, increasing digitization of information services and media content is inevitable, as is the subsequent convergence of the technologies carrying the digitized products. Yet the instigator behind all of this rapid change in the information-based media and communications industries, the Internet, despite affecting the production and distribution portions of media and communications content, still has proven illusory regarding profits and strategic advantages for certain traditional media players.

Partnerships amongst media, Internet technology and broadband distribution firms are transitory steps meant to test business viabilities in the digital arena. Ultimately, should the broadband product be valuable (or disruptive) enough to media firms, the product owner will be acquired to compliment the media firms' content offerings.

## Consequences of Digital Convergence

The idea of convergence has been coming in and out of fashion for more than two decades. The process can be cast in religious terms. A band of early prophets set out a vision. Afterwards, a succession of messiah-technologies appeared that promised to realize the great vision.

Convergence, the digital takeover of communication and information, produces a new kind of interchangeability and interconnectedness among different media forms. The rise of digital media results in:

— the coming together, in a single application or service, of information content from telephony, sound broadcasting, television, motion pictures, photography, printed text publishing, and electronic money;

— a growing degree of overlap in the functions that can be performed by different telecommunications networks; and

— a growth in the interactivity and interoperability and of different networks and information appliances in the home and the office.

The proposition that all modes of communication and information will converge into a digital nexus has been circulating for about twenty-five years. One of the earliest expressions of the idea came from Nicholas Negroponte, a technologist and founder of MIT's Media Lab. In 1978, he used three overlapping circles to represent the technologies of computing, printing, and broadcasting.

The most rapid growth and innovation, he argued, could be found in the area where the three intersected. Negroponte had overlooked the telephone system, but simultaneously, telecommunications analysts were developing their own language of merging technologies. Harvard's Anthony Oettinger, coined the ugly neologism "compunications" to express the growing overlap of computing and telecommunications.

French writers Nora and Minc independently came up with the more graceful "telematique" to express the same idea. Neither term ever quite caught on, and to this day the world is still struggling with awkward combinations of terms such as "telecommunications," "information" and "computing" to label the basic technology of the information economy.

Convergence as analyzed here is a combination of two factors: technological improvements in processing power, and the adoption of common protocols and standards. To some, the term convergence suggests a marriage or a coming together of different technologies or industries. That image is a misleading one.

Convergence is really a takeover of all forms of media by one technology: digital computers, a technological system with solid-state integrated circuits (ICs) at its core, supplemented by photonic components (lasers and optical fibers) and applications of mathematical information theory.

The ability of digital systems to handle multimedia content at lower and lower costs is a product of exponential progress in the processing power and memory of ICs. This, in turn, depends on the ability to increase the density of transistors on a single IC chip.

## Law of Moore

The first integrated circuits were fabricated in 1960. In 1971, the Intel Corporation created the first microprocessor by placing an entire computer central processing unit on a single silicon chip the size of a fingernail. From 1960 until today, the transistor density of a single IC chip has doubled approximately every two years. This phenomenon was first identified by Gordon Moore of Intel in 1968, and became known as "Moore's law."

A corollary of Moore's law states that the cost of an IC is approximately proportional to the square root of IC complexity, which means that the cost of carrying out any particular task with ICs will be cut in half about once every two years.

The link between the progress of media convergence and advances in integrated circuitry is well established in the literature. The spreading applications of ICs are not responses to a world of digital content and networks. On the contrary, content and networks have gone digital in order to avail themselves of the power of ICs.

For example, most of the recent advances in digital video were not possible until a frame of digitized video could be stored on a single chip. The Internet's ability to deliver voice and video signals to PC users required upgrades in the processing speed and memory of a typical PC and increases in the bandwidth and processing speed of the network and its routers.

Likewise, the addition of data screens to mobile telephones, and the adoption of CD-ROMs as a common storage medium for PC data, recorded music, and movies, both stem from a common root: lower priced and more powerful computer and laser components. The pace of convergence has thus been largely determined by the operation of Moore's law.

Moore's law has held true for thirty-five years. The most conservative estimates project that the rate of improvement will begin to level off around 2005. Moore himself predicts that advances in circuit complexity will begin to bump up against physical limits around the year 2010. Some technologists, however, believe that current rates of change may continue 3 even longer if transistors operated by a single electron, which exist already in the laboratory, can be successfully commercialized.

Whichever forecast turns out to be correct, the technological progress supporting digital convergence still has a long way to go. Gordon Moore stated: Even with the level of technology we can extrapolate fairly easily-a few more generations-we can imagine putting a billion transistors on a chip. A billion transistors is mind-boggling. Our most advanced chips in design today will have less than 10 million transistors. So, we're talking about a hundred times the complexity of today's chips. Exploiting that level of technology...could keep us busy for a century.

Semiconductor industry expert Michael Slater provides a more specific assessment of the capabilities of a billion-transistor chip: A single such chip could have dozens of processors, each with several times the complexity of today's most advanced devices, plus several megabytes of cache for each. Running at several gigahertz, the chip could include a video and 3D graphics system, peripheral controllers, a network interface modem, and so forth.

A system could be built with everything in the fastest workstation today, including memory, in a single chip. A $10 microcontroller will be faster than the fastest microprocessor today and have a full set of peripherals. With that many transistors on a chip, a desktop computer will be able to store an entire copy of a high-definition movie in RAM and manipulate it in real time.

In effect, video content will be moved about and manipulated as easily as e-mail is today. But raw technological power is only part of the convergence story. Often overlooked is the fact that digital convergence also implies a process of settling upon common protocols and technical standards for data interchanges. This is a predominantly socio-economic process, not a technical one.

It involves the coordinated adoption of compatible technology platforms by a critical mass of producers and consumers. That process is affected by network externalities and product life-cycles. So, in many ways, the progress of digital convergence is a story of the rise and fall of specific standards that were designed to bring together various media forms.

And as economic theory on standardization has demonstrated, such processes are path-dependent, and may be "tipped" into one of various possible equilibria by chance events. Many observers - especially the telephone companies who had developed it -thought that the ISDN standard was going to be the incarnation of convergence.

ISDN was developed by the ITU starting in the late 1970s, and released as a mature standard in the first half of the 1980s. In promoting ISDN, telephone companies used the same promise of voice and data integration, including hints of the eventual inclusion of video. But of course ISDN never took hold.

The telephone companies priced it as a premium service and did not commit themselves to a wholesale upgrade of their networks. Implementation was complex, and in the US, where data communication was most developed in the 1980s, the AT&T divestiture's fragmentation of the operating companies made the costs of cooperation higher and thus the development of different "flavors" of ISDN inevitable.

One obvious limitation on the success of ISDN is that most consumers simply didn't know what it was supposed to do for them. In the 1980s, many data communication applications generally were built around proprietary equipment and protocols, such as IBM's SNA standard. There was still a lack of integration at the corporate and product development levels between telephone companies and computer companies.

ISDN was no match for open standards, such as the IEEE's Ethernet, that could be directly managed and implemented by companies building LANs, rather than acquired from a third-party vendor.

Indeed, the tremendous success of Ethernet demonstrated that open, non-proprietary standards enjoyed key advantages in the marketplace. Although it was inferior to the proprietary token-ring standard in purely technical ways, it nevertheless gave buyers more security and lower prices. Its initial success was reinforced as network designers and implementers became more familiar and comfortable with its features, leading to a bigger market, lower prices, more product development and diversity.

One of the key factors is that a very large portion of intra-organizational networking has evolved as private networks; i.e., networks that were put together on a decentralized basis by the users themselves, not as large-scale service offered by a public carrier. This meant that compatibility and convergence had to take shape as bottom-up processes, rather than being imposed from the top down.

The cost of bandwidth over long distances creates very powerful economic incentives for most private and public networks to "converge" all forms of traffic onto high-speed backbones. The Synchronous Optical Network (SONET) standard (known as SDH in Europe) is a time-division multiplexing technique developed by long distance carriers to combine many channels of voice traffic onto a single, high-bandwidth link.

But it is a digital standard, so that data traffic can also be mixed into the bitstream. The problem is that it must first be fitted into the 64 kbps channel standard developed for voice traffic. In general, circuit-switching and time-divison multiplexing are less efficient ways of carrying data traffic, which is bursty rather than continuous and may require greater bandwidth than a single voice channel.

Thus throughout most of the 1990s, high speed voice-oriented backbones often used different standards to the data backbones in corporate and telephone company networks, which were more likely to be based on data-oriented standards such as frame relay. Furthermore, these data-oriented standards were designed to have limited functionality. They were not designed to be broad-based convergence technologies.

The Internet protocol suite (TCP/IP) was designed to support internetworking. This means that it permits the interconnection of multiple networks that use different hardware and communication conventions. TCP/IP is a form of packet-based data communications, which routes small chunks of data from one machine to another based on address information carried in the packet.

By the early 1990s, TCP/IP had begun to emerge as a very powerful solution to the data communication problems posed by the world of heterogeneous standards and equipment used in private networks. Like Ethernet, it was an open, non-proprietary standard.

The basic technology of TCP/IP has survived almost two decades of exponential growth. During the past three years, TCP/IP has become the "protocol of convergence" for many companies and services. Internet telephony, and the streaming of video and audio on the Internet, is now commonplace, although the quality of service offered rarely matches that offered by networks based on more traditional standards. One of the weaknesses of IP is in the area of mobile communications.

Asynchronous Transfer Mode (ATM) was the telephone companies' response to the rise of the Internet.

It attempted to combine the benefits of the circuit-switched telephone networks (dedicated connections, guaranteed quality of service) with the benefits of a packet-based communication standard (which used bandwidth more efficiently).

Unlike TCP/IP, ATM fits all data into a uniform packet size (known as a cell) and uses statistical multiplexing over virtual circuits. The uniform packet size makes it easier for ATM to provide isochronous services, such as voice or video, that do not tolerate delay. ATM can carry TCP/IP traffic, but one must chop up TCP/IP packets and fit them into a series of ATM cells.

Carriers in the United States have recently begun to offer ATM backbone services. From the above one can begin to appreciate the complexity of converging real standards and equipment. In fact, a given user may employ many of these standards simultaneously.

An Ethernet Local Area Network can be connected to the Internet via a ATM Wide Area Network, and once on the Internet may end up running over a SONET link. The most significant question is whether any one of these standards, most notably ATM or an improved TCP/IP, can eventually handle all the different service qualities and features that a given user might demand.

## Market Structure of Digital Media

The business implications of digital convergence are profound. The economic organization of some of the world's largest, fastest-growing industries is being transformed. No one can predict precisely what shape this transformation will take. Nevertheless, some vital aspects of a significant change in market structure are already visible. Twenty years ago, most people thought that digitalization would lead to a gigantic consolidation and merger of all media infrastructures into one vertically integrated monopoly.

The "electronic nightmare" scenario projected that media would converge into a horrifying combination of the post office, Microsoft, broadcast networks, and the telephone company. In fact, something much closer to the opposite is happening. Cheap, abundant processing power is promoting disintegration and specialization along the communications value chain. In computers, telecommunications, and broadcasting, successful firms are moving away from end-to-end, vertical integration to focus on specialized, horizontal segments of the market.

Devices, distribution channels, and applications are becoming more diverse and specialized as well as more interoperable. The result is not a "unification" of broadcasting, computing, and telecommunications, but a completely new media ecology. This section identifies some of the key features of this change.

## Analogue Media

Prior to digitalization, different electronic communication services formed discrete chains of components that restricted distinct kinds of communication and content to specific distribution networks and terminals. In many cases, especially the telephone and telegraph systems, the supplying firm was vertically integrated over the entire chain.

Even when the supplying firm itself was not vertically integrated over the entire component chain, the vertical structure was maintained by technological barriers that prevented information from being easily transferred from one system to another. Telephony, telegraphy, broadcasting, motion pictures, publishing, money, and documents were all vertically integrated chains linking a specific kind of content, distribution network, and terminal.

There were some cross-linkages between these vertical chains, especially in the transmission segment. But for the most part they operated as separate systems. In telephone communication a single, vertically integrated monopoly supplied end-to-end service. Documents, data, money, financial transactions, and publications were largely restricted to the media of printed paper and physical distribution via a monopoly post office.

The telegraph provided an important link between the worlds of telecommunication and print/paper, but telegraph transmissions relied on manual input, which severely limited their capacity. There were no credit cards and very limited forms of electronic funds transfer.

Broadcast receivers and playback systems for recorded sound were also discrete technological systems. The real source of the vertical structure was not the content-carrier segment of the chain. Television and radio broadcast signals, voice signals, photographs, and text could all be converted into analogue electronic signals and carried by trunk telecommunication networks.

The segregation of services took place primarily at the input and output terminal. Final distribution to users involved application-specific devices that could neither communicate with devices from other content-carrier chains, nor convert information into and out of other formats. Thus, convergence was limited by the limited processing power of end-user terminals.

Compared to today, the technology that was needed to generate, process, convert, store and retrieve signals automatically was delicate, primitive, and expensive. It was, therefore, concentrated in organizations remote from the user, so that economies could be made and technical standards could be tightly controlled. It was also not standardized across media.

## PCs and the Horizontal Shift

The early computer industry adopted this vertical structure. Until the late 1970s, it consisted of a few large, vertically integrated manufacturers. Each manufacturer designed its own system around a proprietary architecture. They often developed and produced their own semiconductor devices for memory and processing, and employed their own applications software.

Manufacturers also directly controlled the sales and distribution of their machines. By the late 1970s, rapidly developing microprocessor technology put all the basic processing functions of a computer on a single chip. Computers began to be assembled around a microprocessor, supplemented by readily available components such as memory chips, I/O controllers, disc drives, and peripherals.

IBM's introduction of the PC in 1981 inadvertently reinforced this modular approach to computer manufacture, and ultimately led to the destruction of the vertical structure in computer manufacturing. Because of the competitive threat represented by Apple Computer and other microcomputer manufacturers, IBM needed to enter the market quickly.

It therefore abandoned its normal procedures, which relied on methodical, in-house development of a closed, proprietary architecture. Instead, IBM introduced an open architecture and off-the-shelf components, and held very little intellectual property protection over the result. As a result, the product and its architecture were easily imitated.

The result is now apparent to all. With the exception of Apple, the entire personal computer industry standardized around the IBM PC system architecture. Clone manufacturers took over 75-80 per cent of the PC market. Their competition and rapid innovations created constant pressure to lower prices and improve features.

A new, more specialized industry structure emerged, characterized by competition between firms with strong positions in one of five horizontal segments of production. These five segments are:

1) microprocessors;
2) manufacture of computer platforms;
3) Operating systems software;
4) Applications software; and
5) Distribution.

Vertical links between one or two of these segments remain. Microsoft, for example, has leveraged its strength in operating systems to take over the lion's share of the applications software market. IBM still has significant positions in four of the segments, and its acquisition of Lotus in 1995 extended its position in applications software.

Even so, market share is usually won or lost on the basis of competitiveness in horizontal segments. IBM PCs, for example, generally use Intel microprocessors. The strongest positions (e.g., those of Microsoft, Intel, Compaq) have generally been achieved precisely because the supplier specialized in one horizontal segment and did not try to extend that control too far up or down the value chain. End-to-end vertical integration has been almost entirely banished from the marketplace.

The decline of Apple Computer's market share, its alliance with IBM and its licensing of independent manufacturers in the 1990s, represent the final stages of this transition.

The pattern experienced by the computer industry in the 1980s is now spreading throughout the telecommunication and media industries. The process is driven by the growing power of microprocessors and a shift in the distribution of information processing and storage power toward the end user, which leads to more open standards and interfaces across horizontal segments. The vertical segmentation of media is being replaced by a converged digital media market composed of five distinct horizontal segments. These segments can be defined as

1) Content creation and production;
2) Service packaging;
3) Carriage;

4) Software; and

5) Equipment.

Content refers to the creation and production of symbolic material that has been encoded in a particular format. Motion pictures, television programming, newspaper articles, book manuscripts, recorded music, and the information on a Web site are all examples of content. So are human speech and money. In general, content refers to material that consumers value in and of itself, either for its entertainment value or for its educational, news, or exchange value.

Packaging refers to the intermediary function wherein different types of content and/or software are assembled into a product or service bundle. Packagers reduce search costs for consumers and also provide a quality control and assurance function. Carriage refers to the business of distributing or transporting information.

Telephone transmission networks, cable TV systems, or, more generically, optical fibre, co-axial copper cable, communication via radio frequencies, or vehicular transportation are examples of different types of carriage. Equipment manufacturing refers to hardware devices that enable telecommunication and information processing.

Software, the stored instructions that manipulate or process information in a particular way, is an essential element of the model. Software markets are often bundled with equipment, but nevertheless represent a distinct product.

Desktop applications, switching, routing and network management protocols, browser software, information storage and retrieval protocols, multiplexing and signal compression, search engines, and transaction processing are all examples of software. Software is an input that is present throughout the communication chain, but it is also a discrete market.

## Aspects of Horizontalization

According to traditional natural monopoly theory, monopoly and concentration are products of economies of scale and scope in supply. Digital technology, however, massively increases the economies of scale and scope that can be achieved in the switching, transmission, and storage and duplication of content. Why, then, has the rise of digital media radically undermined monopoly and vertical integration instead of reinforcing it? There are two reasons. One is that mass-produced digital intelligence reduces the social cost of multiple, heterogeneous networks and systems. Or, to put it differently, it radically undermines the advantages of vertical integration. The other reason is that the declining price of intelligence has brought the capital investments needed to acquire it well within the budget constraints of ordinary firms and households.

Reducing the capital intensity of intelligence also reduces the importance of building large-scale organizations that can share its costs among many users. In the old market structure, the five building blocks of the communications value chain were mostly vertically integrated around specific media. A typical broadcaster, for example, produced most of its own content, assembled outsourced content into a service package, and owned and operated its signal transmitter.

Although vertical integration did not extend all the way to the end user's receiving equipment, this gap was filled by rigid government regulations confining transmissions to specific frequency bands and locations and controlling the characteristics of broadcast terminals. Likewise, telecommunication companies manufactured the terminal; built, owned, and operated the carriage network; and centrally controlled and managed the network intelligence.

Service packages and specialized applications of network capabilities were developed internally by the telecommunication companies. To understand the new structure of media it is first necessary to understand what sustained the old one. The vertical, monopolistic form of communication media was basically a product of the high price of intelligence.

In the era of electromechanical telephone switching, for example, increases in the scale of the network placed heavy demands on network intelligence. Additional information processing power could only be purchased with disproportional inputs of capital and labor. Increases in the size and complexity of telephone switching offices beyond a certain point created major diseconomies of growth.

Under these conditions, any attempt to interconnect multiple, competing networks, or to support heterogeneous forms of terminal equipment, added greatly to the expense of the network. More diversity and complexity meant disproportionate increases in the physical facilities and labor resources needed to run the system. The viability of competition in telecommunication can be directly related to technological changes that reduced the price of processing power.

With electromechanical technology there was only two ways to have competing telephone systems and, at the same time, allow all telephone users to be able to call each other. One was to let some users rent two access lines and telephone sets (demand-side duplication). The other was to require the competing systems to interconnect. The latter option (supply-side duplication) was as expensive as the first, for it created a duplicate trunk network, greatly enlarged the size and complexity of the switchboards, and also required major increases in the size of central offices' staff.

In digital electronic networks, interconnection of additional networks requires more intelligence, but only a little more hardware and very little additional labor. The complex exchanges of information required to interconnect independently managed networks can be achieved rapidly and automatically, through software protocols. Processing power acts as a direct substitute for the duplication of physical facilities and labor.

When intelligence is very expensive, it must be shared among multiple users. Its application must be conserved, restricted to the most important functions. The capital investment it represents can only come from a large organization and can only be recovered by spreading its costs across a significant portion of the population.

When intelligence is abundant, sharing economies become less important; control and convenience rise in significance. As high levels of processing power come within the budget constraint of households and businesses, there is greater economic tolerance of diversity, duplication, and "waste" for the sake of convenience, customization, and control. It is the same in other industries.

From the standpoint of simple sharing economies, for example, a public bus or train is always more efficient than a private automobile. But the wealthier a society becomes, the more its consumers purchase automobiles and avoid public transport. The structural consequences of the declining price of intelligence can be summarized as follows.

— There is greater fungibility among the different components of the communication chain. That is, an end user or service provider can more easily mix and match a product or service from one horizontal segment with the products and services from any other segment to configure a communication service. Weaker vertical links among specific applications means that competition is more focused on achieving market share in specific horizontal segments of the chain.

— As the price of intelligence drops, it becomes more evenly distributed throughout the chain. Terminal equipment, once the "dumbest" part of the communication chain, has become vastly more intelligent. The concentration of intelligence in central switching offices and bureaucratic management hierarchies has gradually eroded. Instead, end users have asserted ownership and control over terminals and on-premises networks.

— There is divergence, not convergence, in each horizontal segment. The horizontal shift is naturally accompanied by a growth of specialization and diversity in the market as a whole. A standard feature of intense competition is that it forces competitors to differentiate their products and services. The market becomes more responsive to slight variations in demand. This trend is evident in all five segments. In data terminals there are still mainframes and PCs, but there are also smart cards, notebooks, palmtops, organizers, and PDAs.

Telephones and pagers come in all shapes and sizes, representing different ways of handling technical and economic tradeoffs between cost, bandwidth, portability, quality, mobility, and power utilization. There is greater differentiation of audiovisual playback devices, ranging from the tiny, portable car TV to the gigantic home projection screen.

In carriage, digital convergence has made different kinds of networks better substitutes for each other. But we do not see the carriage market collapsing into a single infrastructure; rather, competing infrastructures are proliferating, each targeted at a range of applications in which it holds a competitive advantage, and often working in a complementary fashion with other infrastructures.

Thus, there are new fixed local networks; private LANs and WANs; many new public wireless local networks; multiple trunk networks for long distance; new, redundant cables for international communication; simultaneous growth of satellite and cable alternatives to terrestrial broadcasting; and so on.

In content production the same growth of diversity is present. A standard result of economic analysis was that the mass-oriented, "lowest common denominator" quality of television and radio programming was a function of limitations on the number of channels and the broadcast medium's reliance on advertising support.

Digital, interactive media are overcoming both limitations. Video, on-line, and audio content can increasingly be ordered and paid for on a transactional basis, and need not be supported solely by advertising. And the number of channels is increasing. The overall market for content, therefore, is beginning to look as diverse and fragmented as the market for printed publications.

The market for service packagers and software is also increasingly diverse and specialized. The vertical structure of the telecommunications industry first began to disintegrate thirty years ago. The first step was the detachment of terminal equipment markets from the market for network services. This process was driven by the desire of electronic equipment manufacturers and users to pry open markets that were foreclosed by telephone companies' monopoly control of the access infrastructure.

The creation of a standardized interface between the public network and the customer's equipment facilitated end user ownership of telephone handsets and PBXs, and promoted freer competition in terminal equipment markets. The rise of competition in long distance markets in the USA eventually led to an attempt to create an analogous standardized interface between local and long distance segments of the network.

Without electronic switching intelligence, this would have been economically intractable. Another important development was the emergence of a distinction between the physical network and network intelligence in the form of "value-added services." This distinction had its roots in the emergence of computer networks that employed the telephone network for carriage but "added value" in the form of processing or storage.

Despite this trend away from vertical integration, the prospect of converging telecommunication and audiovisual media in the early 1990s was interpreted by many businesses and analysts as an opportunity for telephone and cable companies to reassert the old vertical structure. Telephone companies, threatened with competition in their traditional markets, began to view broadband networks offering interactive entertainment as the key to their future growth.

The Internet's rapid diffusion could be directly attributed to its features of decentralized innovation, open, non-proprietary standards and the absence of end-to-end integration. The modular, horizontally organized Internet market thoroughly undermined the fundamental assumptions of the telco-cable approach to interactive media development.

In 1996 telephone companies, including Hong Kong Telecom IMS, stampeded into the Internet Service Provider (ISP) market, often achieving great success. Cable TV companies kept pace by developing cable modems that would allow cable customers to gain high-speed access to the Internet. Whether they knew it or not, these changes amounted to a strategic repositioning away from vertical integration towards their horizontal strengths in carriage.

Almost all of the merger activity that has taken place in the United States since the passage of the 1996 Telecommunications Act has been in horizontal segments of the market. Radio and TV broadcasting chains have acquired other radio and TV broadcasters; telephone companies have acquired other telephone companies; content giants have acquired other content originators.

At the same time, there is dramatic evidence of the failure of vertically-oriented approaches to convergence and consolidation. No major mergers between telephone company giants and cable multiple system operators have succeeded. AT&T's self-divestiture of Lucent and NCR established clear separations between its business lines in computer manufacturing and services, telecommunication service, and equipment manufacturing.

A convergent media market structure already exists in the Internet. Worldwide, the Internet industry is beginning to experiment with a fully converged environment in which television sets, telephones, and various digital devices besides PCs can be used to access and navigate the 'Net.

This, of course, is what convergence is all about-and there is no doubt that the meeting point for this change will be the Internet rather than traditional cable TV or voice telephone systems. Thus, the Internet must be viewed as a bandwidth-constrained, administratively immature version of the fully digital media of the future.

It represents the future of broadcasting and telecommunications as well as the future of networked computing. As such, its economic features offer important insights into the market structures and policy problems created by digital convergence. Key features of market structure include the following:

### *Multimedia Capability*

The Internet can carry and deliver all modes of content on an interactive basis. Old distinctions between publishing, broadcasting, and telecommunications have already lost their meaning on the Internet. The segmentation of voice, video, and data traffic is also undermined, although not abolished. The Internet currently offers access to news content, mail and document distribution, financial services, photos and graphics, various forms of electronic commerce and digital money, games, real-time voice and music clips, and even some limited clips of real-time video.

In addition, it has created new forms of media such as chat rooms, MUDs, search engines, and browsers. The Internet's multimedia capabilities are still limited by congestion, low-bandwidth access to residences, and the presence of older chipsets in many home and office computers. Over time, however, new administrative arrangements, better pricing mechanisms, the expanding power of ICs, and equipment upgrades will reduce these barriers.

### *Disintegration*

The Internet is largely disintegrated in structure. TCP/IP, the protocol on which it is based, is an open, non-proprietary standard. There are clear demarcations between the markets for terminal equipment, browser software, local carriage, backbone carriage, service packagers, and content producers. Suppliers concentrate on maximizing their competence and market share in one or two of these horizontal segments of the market.

The environment of vertical disintegration has a powerful impact on the flexibility of service configuration and the possibilities for service innovation. Packagers and intermediaries can "mix and match" service components to create a product. Internet services may be advertising supported, subscription-based, free, pay per view, or a combination of these options; their delivery architecture includes both "pull" and "push" interfaces. The old broadcast-telecommunication categories are totally irrelevant in this environment.

An important corollary of disintegration is that end-users in businesses and residences can assert ownership over terminal equipment, in-premises distribution, content, and software interfaces. Service providers must compete not only with other service providers, but with equipment manufacturers. The consumer can control when to lease and when to buy. This creates further pressure toward open, "plug and play" standards and a disintegrated value chain.

### *A Borderless Market*

The falling cost of bandwidth and processing power makes national boundaries increasingly irrelevant in determining the features of digital media. Unlike traditional telephony, there is no "distance premium" on the Internet and no regulatory regime, like the international settlements system, that makes data movements pay special taxes for crossing international borders.

Multimedia content can be distributed globally and, via electronic commerce, services and products can be consumed from any point. It will become increasingly difficult-and counterproductive-for governments to monitor and control the movement of bits. A regime of increasingly free trade in information and telecommunication services and content seems inevitable.

When entire motion pictures can be transmitted in encrypted form over international lines in a few seconds, and when Internet users can experience or download pictures, music or videos hosted on computers far outside their home country's jurisdiction, the concept of broadcasting laws and regulations that restrict ownership to nationals or prescribe the kind of content that people can view within the country cannot survive for long.

Convergence of media and wider participation in communication underlie the global information revolution now permeating the Arab Middle East and bypassing efforts of nearly all governments of the region to control the print and broadcast media. The information revolution in the Middle East features more of everything: media, especially transnational media, information, and erosion of boundaries to communication carefully erected by state monopolies.

It particularly erodes attempts to limit public discourse to the promotion of acceptable views. New technologies, the convergence of satellite broadcasting and the Internet, a multiplication of actors in a widening public realm, and generational change are bringing forward the region's first cohort raised on television with increasing numbers adept in the Internet. The Internet is a global phenomenon, but with a distinct regional profile.

Dabbagh Information Technology in Dubai estimates that less than one percent of households in the Arab Middle East subscribe to Internet services, rising to three percent in some Gulf countries, with growth rates in the low double digits. The typical respondent in DIT's surveys is younger, more educated, and far more likely to be both professional and male than in the US or Europe.

Internet growth in the Arab Middle East is primarily connected to commercial concerns, in comparison to the leading role played by universities and research in the US. While sponsored as industrial development by the government in Egypt, throughout the region the Internet is more commonly a child of telecommunications concerns and the media arms of commercial conglomerates.

A few research institutes had early connections, but commercial interests have brought the region on-line as an additional dimension of distribution and marketing. Part of the reason is that the technology is readily available and largely off-the-shelf, but the costs to businesses are low in comparison to the economic costs and other impediments to individual users.

Actual consumers of Internet services in the region to date have largely been firms, and a panoply of firms has emerged to provide everything from physical connection to site-design and hosting to other support services. These are commonly spin-offs from established telecommunications, trading, and media concerns in both public and private sectors.

For "end" users, the cost of equipment and connections, limited infrastructure, and the overwhelmingly English language medium have kept the Internet beyond reach for all but a handful of scientists and engineers at selected government research institutes, international companies for whom the information superhighway is a potential place of business, and visionaries in official positions and the private sector.

Convergence, however, is changing this picture. Technologically, there is no bar to convergence. The

Internet fundamentally depends on telecommunications capacity, which has been a rising throughout most of the region and especially in Gulf countries. In the past year, satellite broadcasters have offered or bought Internet services. Arabia.On.Line, one of the first Arab World Wide Web sites, survived the demise of its parent, Byte Middle East, and is now part-owned by Prince al-Waleed bin Talal, the Saudi media mogul with interests in Arab Radio and Television, ZakSat, and mobile telephones.

Other Gulf broadcasters offering international fare have announced Internet services in connection with satellite television: the Showtime satellite network of Gulf DTH will offer some 600 websites through the ZakNet subsidiary of ZakSat. Today's convergence is in applications, particularly around entertainment. AROL, for instance, has added sports to its daily offering of regional political, commercial, and technological news for a business audience.

The most striking example is Saudi Arabia's adoption of an entertainment model for regulating public access to the Internet, which must meet standards of broadcasting "propriety ." Moreover, the structure of the Saudi services, through a government controlled gateway, is similar to schemes for Satellite Master Antenna Systems and Multi Channel Microwave Distribution to replace individually owned satellite dishes, nominally banned in the Kingdom. A glance at the dish-equipped rooftops of any Middle Eastern city attests to the penetration of satellite television.

As important as the rising number of receivers is the rising number and variety of senders, of which al-Jazeera is only the most prominent. By comparison to entertainment-and-sports formats favored by ArabSat members, al-Jazeera is the first to feature full-time news and discussion and serious competition for MBC, a formerly Lebanese broadcaster reborn on a CNN model and relocated to London. Perhaps al-Jazeera's most popular show is "al-Ittijah al-Mu'akis", which has served as an open forum for political debate and attracted the ire of Arab governments unaccustomed to such competition in a medium they have heretofore dominated.

The real change is not the emergence of alternative voices in public media, but their sheer variety. This is the Internet model. From modest beginnings as a showcase for the technology and its commercial possibilities for image advertising, the Internet has had a role in expanding the media environment.

As Jon Alterman notes in a recent study, among the first beneficiaries of the Internet in the Middle East have been journalists and the press. Most of the transnational Arab press, nearly all of the English editions of regional publications, and a rising number of the Arabic ones are now on-line. Their individual presences collectively constitute a new community of communication that is transnational, open to more participants, and interactive in a way that traditional broadcasting has not been.

Until now, broadcasting and electronic media in the Middle East generally narrowed rather than widened the possibilities for communication. As government monopolies, they were instruments of state-building, and still are for those with dirigiste inclinations, now in the guise of education, economic development, and providing a controlled space for religious broadcasting. A new information regime is emerging that magnifies what has been a minor presence and arm's length relationship.

Many Middle Eastern governments tolerate a degree of experimentation abroad that is anathema at home and in Arabic. Free expression at the margins provides a safety valve and a way of keeping tabs on opponents and alternatives at a safe distance from local arenas. This "distancing" is breaking down, not just as those arenas are penetrated, but more importantly as the number of conversations multiplies and find their way into public media and wider circulation.

Underlying these trends are more fundamental ones of demographic change. The average tenure of contemporary Arab regimes is approaching 18 years and converging on the median age of populations that are increasingly educated and increasingly urban. Old habits, such as the "honor code" that the Arab States Broadcasting Union urges on al-Jazeera, meet new realities that include a several decades long rise in mass education, particularly mass higher education, and reconnection with the Arab diaspora that together erode old monopolies on information and communication.

In this context, technologies from cassette recording to satellite TV to the Internet accelerate communication, bypass gatekeepers, reduce the social distance between sender and receiver, segment markets, and give voice and place to special, even to passing, interests. The first generation of mass media, such as government broadcasting monopolies, now faces the competition of more user-friendly media that began with cassette recorders and are now joined by "narrowcasting" and its ultimate (for now) expression in the Internet.

This retail technology brings into the public arena conventions and practices of face-to-face communication that mass communications had relegated to a "private" realm, expanding their reach and what is in public. This may be more significant in the longer term than the possibilities for media celebrity as the public sphere is enriched not just by more players but by more conversations and more ways for consumers/recipients to recognize themselves and their lives in public discourse.

An early result is a more diverse Arab media culture, which has been dominated by political reporting and ideological commentary. Mass media facilitated a journalism that is part of the political culture on which it reports; new media, by bringing more of society into public discourse, facilitate a broader-based journalism.

Other identities figure prominently in new media, as cassette recordings circulate not only sermons of prominent preachers but also folk music and recitations, or local and even neighborhood television stations feature neighbors addressing local and even neighborhood issues, or the Internet, which first interests professionals. Another result is that indigenous forms come the fore and surface tensions between local diversities and would-be uniformitarians.

While al-Jazeera has made an enormous splash, attracting viewers across the region, many of whom call in to talk shows, and the Internet currently has a limited base, ultimately the Internet is the more important. It is the model for post-mass media marked by audience fragmentation, diversity, seeking over receiving; and in these terms, al-Jazeera is TV on an Internet model.

## Cross-Media Rules

Over the last decade or so developments in information

technology have enabled the digitisation and transmission of video, image, sound and text. Television, telecommunications and computer services are becoming integrated, or converging. This process is said to affect the cross-media laws by:

— increasing the number of media outlets to such an extent that ownership limits are no longer required to preserve media diversity, and

— blurring the boundaries between services, so that regulatory distinctions become meaningless.

The major effect of the cross-media provisions of the Broadcasting Services Act 1992 is to prevent the common ownership of newspapers, television or radio broadcasting licences that serve the same region. The purpose of the legislation is to encourage diversity in the ownership of the most influential forms of the commercial media: the daily press and free-to-air television and radio.

The justification for the rules is that the effective functioning of a democracy requires a diverse ownership of the daily mass media to ensure that public life be reported in a fair and open manner.

While new media penetration is still well below that of radio and television, it is increasing rapidly. The number of households with access to the Internet increased by 49 per cent between February and November 1998. After levelling off in early 1998, pay TV subscriptions also appear to have increased sharply. Has this rapid growth in pay TV and Internet households weakened the case for cross-media controls by providing a greater diversity of media outlets that report on Australian current affairs?

Theoretically, the Internet should have added to media diversity by eliminating the need for large capital outlays by new entrants. However, the operating costs of maintaining a news organisation together with the lack of Internet advertising revenue have ensured that no new competitor has emerged to challenge the traditional mass media, which can transfer its existing content to the Internet at little extra cost.

The Internet's main contribution to media diversity has been to increase the possible influence of the print media by improving its household access. This could be seen as a reason for retaining the cross-media rules, rather than abandoning them. It has been claimed that convergence will blur the boundaries between the different forms of media: TV programs will be viewable on the computer, while Internet style services will be displayed on the television.

The distinction between television programs and 'datacasting' services combining text, image and sound may become difficult to define. While these effects are not yet a reality, the transition to digital television will soon provide the capacity for the broadcasting of these services to Australian households. However, it is unlikely that this will significantly alter the nature of the household data market in the short to medium term, as it is now dominated by the computer.

The digital transition commences on 1 January 2001 in metropolitan areas and 1 January 2004 in regional areas, but it will not be until eight years after those dates that digital equipment is required in order to continue watching television. In contrast, computers are frequently used in 35.8 per cent of Australian households and 18.6 per cent of households are already connected to the Internet.

The connection rate for upper income earners, who would most likely be the first to buy digital television, is 41.5 per cent. The distinctions between current Internet services and broadcasting are still quite clear: the former are delivered interactively through a unique connection to an individual household while the latter are broadcast to anyone who has the necessary receiving equipment.

The fact that television broadcasters may gradually move into the household data market is not in itself a reason for abandoning the cross-media rules. As the cross media provisions of the Broadcasting Services Act 1992 are not yet obsolete, it might be argued that they should not be repealed on the basis of a putative future when the practical consequences of their abolition could be a significant reduction in media diversity.

# 6

# Assessment of Communication Components

Digital broadcasting will do more to shape the industry into the next millennium than any other factor. Analogue television use of the spectrum is very wasteful, digital transmission presents an opportunity to open up large areas of spectrum for other users, including personal communications.

The Broadcasting Act 1996 initiated the creation of six terrestrial Multiplexes, bundles of frequencies, which can be split into at least three channels each for services that need little capacity. Five of the channels derived from the six multiplexes will be set aside for the use of the five existing terrestrial analogue services.

The key difficulty facing digital broadcasters, is the need to tempt viewers to buy the set-top box needed to receive digital broadcasts on their analogue television sets. The main digital terrestrial competitor and rival to BSkyB is ONdigital. Jointly owned by Carlton and Granada, it uses BBC and Flextech for content and launched its own digital terrestrial service on 1

November 1998. A number of cable companies are also intending to launch digital services, among them, for instance, Cable and Wireless which plans to launch digital services by the end of 1999.

With only ONdigital and BSkyB's digital services currently operating the final shape of digital television in the UK is not yet finalised and may yet be subject alteration. However, by the end of 1999 there will be three digital platforms offering commercial digital services.

Terrestrial, satellite and cable television operators will be offering viewers a broad range of services. DAB is the name given to a digital radio transmission system. DAB allows sound, text and data to be transmitted digitally through either terrestrial radio frequencies or via satellite. DAB could prove to be the most significant issue to face the commercial radio sector since its inception.

There are serious problems still to be addressed. However, some companies are ready to support the advent of digital radio. In October 1998 three new national digital radio stations were allocated, after the UK's sole national commercial digital radio multiplex was handed to the Digital One consortium.

Digital One expects to be broadcasting 10 digital commercial radio services from 1 October 1999, including the three existing national commercial stations, Classic FM, Virgin and Talk, and seven new channels. Related text data services will also be tested to support programmes and advertising.

The advent of digital television and radio services will offer operators the opportunity to open up new revenue streams such as pay-per-view (PPV). This has already brought significant financial benefits to the non-terrestrial. So far, PPV via pay-TV has mainly been used for one-off sporting or major entertainment events that are prohibitively expensive to either produce or buy the programme rights to.

Sport has been and continues to be where PPV's strength lies. Increasingly it is used for film premiers and first-rate programming and is seen as one of the ways of promoting genuine consumer choice. Television and radio companies have the advantage that they are able to avail themselves of free advertising, including the use of trailers and idents on their own and sister stations.

This therefore is the main way in which the TV companies promote their programming. However, considerable sums are still spent in main media advertising. The total spend for the whole industry to year ending September 1998 was over £102m. The radio industry as a whole spent over £14.5m to the year ending September 1998 on main media advertising ie through TV and national press.

The largest spender during this period was the BBC, whose advertising costs reached over £3.5m. Within the commercial sector, Capitol Radio in conjunction with its other station Capital Gold spent almost as much, with expenditure amounting to over £3.4m. The ITC was established by the Broadcasting Act 1990 to regulate and supervise the activities and operations of commercial television broadcasters.

The ITC has prime responsibility for all aspects of commercial TV. Its main role is that of a licensing and regulatory body. The role of the ITC is becoming increasingly political as competition in broadcasting increases. The decision of the ITC in November 1998 to allow ITV to `move' News at Ten reflects this new attitude to a fast changing broadcasting environment.

The Radio Authority has been the lead regulatory and licensing body for the commercial radio. Over recent months there have been widespread allegations of impropriety and misconduct at the authority. In order to assess consumer reactions to the advent of digital radio and television services, Market Assessment commissioned original research into consumer attitudes.

In October 1998 NOP carried out a survey among a quota sample of 1,001 adults aged over 15. Digital terrestrial attracted a higher level of interest amongst respondents to this survey than either digital satellite, or digital cable. This probably reflects the fact that in the UK most of the population is still totally dependent on terrestrial analogue television for viewing.

The relatively poor performance of digital satellite may be surprising. The cable operators have not really started their own advertising campaign to win digital subscribers; as yet they do not even have a firm launch date for a digital cable service. Furthermore, their limited geographical coverage would limit the size of their natural market.

After the huge marketing campaign launched by BSkyB, to be so far behind ONdigital in terms of consumer interest and so little ahead of the cable sector suggests that BSkyB's continued domination of the pay-television market in the UK is by no means certain. Sky still has significant advantage in the form of first rate subscriber management infrastructure, attractive programming, a high profile brand and an analogue business that will continue to generate a huge turnover for the near future.

Market Assessment believes that Sky is and will remain, for the time being at least, an important force in UK broadcasting, if not the dominant force that it has been since the mid 1990s. With the whole television industry in a state of flux, it is impossible to be certain of the final outcome of current trends. However, Market Assessment anticipates that between 1999 and 2003 the value of the total market will grow by over 40% to £7,443m. Certainly Market Assessment expects that such revenue growth which does occur will be unevenly spread across different market segments.

Convergence is playing a big role in the way broadcasting is changing. Broadcasting-based companies are becoming involved in the provision of telecommunications services by using their own facilities, through cross-ownership of telecommunications companies, or both. There have been a number of large mergers of broadcasting, newspaper, and telecommunications companies in Canada. Some recent example include:

— the publishing company Quebecor Inc. with the cable company Groupe Videotron

— CanWest Global Communications Inc. with the National Post and other major daily newspapers;

Broadcasting is one of the industry groups in Canada's information and cultural sector. According to a Human Resources Development Canada profile on broadcasting, the Canadian public is becoming more technologically literate, and discriminating in their preferences for programming variety, quantity, and quality. This trend is translating into tremendous competition, challenges, and opportunities for the future of broadcasting.

With all the integration or convergence in the media fields, you may have a defined job in television production, but you will likely be involved with several media. A typical day could include reporting a news story, doing a live interview for the morning television broadcast, then writing and submitting the story to a newspaper, and filing it on the Internet.

People who work at television stations indicate that convergence is the key trend in how and what television delivers to its audience. Digital convergence is a multi-billion dollar trend characterized by the merging of computer, graphics, sound, text, video, film, and other communications technologies.

The Cultural Human Resource Council describes digital convergence as the merging of the television, telephone and computer into one media appliance to be used in ways we've never before imagined. Whether you focus on the world of business, education, entertainment, or politics, convergence will push change into every corner of your life.

Competition has permeated and overtaken the world of television. The large number of specialty channels, the impact of satellite delivery, the lure of the Internet, and the growth of e-commerce and shopping on-line have all cut into the number of hours people watch Canadian television. "Content is king," says Craig Roskin of Global.

There are hundreds of specialty channels now and more under development. Information technology allows specialty channels to reach audiences all over the world.

Television audiences are defining themselves more by content than by location. From competition to public demand, and information technology to globalization, many trends are forcing the television industry to stretch horizontally. As a result of these trends, the old media world of radio and television is morphing into multi-platformed, multiple partnership and, multi-media organizations.

It's difficult to say what the future may hold, however, change is most definitely constant and people working in television will need to be creative, analytical, flexible, and open to embracing new technology. Many people in the industry have benefited from a mentor who will broaden their knowledge, teach them the ropes, and take an interest in their career. Examine the several custom made television apprenticeship programs. Visit the National Screen Institute's (NSI) website to find out more about their professional development programs.

The NSI's new "Totally Television" program is being designed to help people working in television continue to sharpen their skills. A national network is offering its employees courses on writing for the Internet, a hybrid of television and newspaper writing styles. People are now entering television work after completing either a technical diploma from a technological institution like NAIT in Edmonton, SAIT in Calgary, or SIAST in Saskatoon; or by earning a university degree.

The degree might be an undergraduate degree in political science, or an applied degree in journalism from institutions, such as the University of Regina, Carleton, or Ryerson Polytechnical University. Many in the field consider internships as a good route because of the valuable experience you will receive. Networking is huge in this industry. Some jobs in television production are:

— Researcher

— Camera Operator

— Journalist/Reporter

— Videographer

— Production Assistant

— Producer

— Director

— Editor

— Marketer

— Video-journalist

— Soundperson

— Scriptwriter

— Network Correspondent.

Senator Fritz Hollings has described the U.S. Telecommunications Act of 1996 as "the Berlin Wall of telecommunications crashing down." As the previous essay makes clear, this landmark legislation removes many of the legal barriers to competition in telephone, cable, and other communications services. In a larger sense, however, the act reinforces trends previously under way in the marketplace.

Driven by the need to expand revenues, U.S. communications companies are devoting more and more of their resources to developing new services and to invading new markets. While businesses' preparations for that invasion are going slower than expected, it remains safe to predict that the communications marketplace will undergo a radical transformation in the years ahead.

Indeed, the industry is already showing signs of tremendous change. The number of corporate mergers, takeovers, and divestitures in recent years has been staggering, and the turmoil is likely to continue into the 21st century. As these companies diversify into new markets, the traditional distinctions among cable, telephone, and satellite companies could disappear entirely. The end result is likely to be a dramatic change in the way that consumers receive different kinds of information, and from whom.

Each local telephone company generally has a monopoly over its service area. As a result, local telephone companies have the most to fear from the introduction of competition. The Telecommunications Act of 1996 removes the local telephone companies' protection as legal monopolies in their respective areas of operation and requires them to allow competitors to use their networks at prices based on their costs. Some companies have taken extraordinary measures to prepare for the competition.

Today these might include Internet access or wireless services. Subject to Federal Communications Commission (FCC) approval, they soon might also include long-distance telephone services. Subject to cost and demand considerations, they might also add video or cable services. Virtually every telephone company has been running marketing trials to determine how best to enter this market and provide video services to the home. They are finding, however, that it is expensive to upgrade their existing telephone networks in a manner that would smoothly handle video signals.

Hence, rather than attempt to build its own cable network or open video system, one RBOC -- USWest --

simply decided to buy Continental Cablevision, the third largest cable operator in the United States. This was allowable under the Telecommunications Act—which banned most buy-outs that would result in one entity controlling both the telecommunication and video lines to consumers' homes—because the two firms did not serve the same market.

It should be technologically and economically easier to provide long-distance service than cable service, if the local telephone companies meet the preconditions specified in the new law. The long-distance market is large, and transmitting telephone calls over long distances is not that different from carrying local calls. GTE and other smaller telephone companies are already in the long-distance market, but the RBOCs must first receive approval from the FCC.

Several RBOCs have already submitted applications to provide long-distance service, although these have been challenged as premature by their competitors who claim that the RBOCs have not yet met the local-competition obligations required by the Telecommunications Act.

The local telephone companies are also investing heavily in wireless licenses in the U.S. and overseas. The RBOCs were among the big winners of the recent auctions for licenses to provide personal communications services (PCS), the next competitor to cellular services. RBOCs have purchased substantial shares of the telephone companies in Mexico and New Zealand and have invested heavily in wireless and cable services in Europe. Several members of the telephone industry are also trying to produce their own television programming "content" so that in the future they will not have to purchase all their video programming from Hollywood movie studios.

But while GTE and the RBOCs are seeking to diversify their revenue sources, none of the new markets on their horizons are likely to be as profitable as their current local telephone operations. Not surprisingly then, they will fight hard to keep the competition out for as long as possible; their court challenges to the FCC's rules implementing the new law's local-competition requirements exemplify this strategy.

But over time, it seems likely that competition for at least some parts of the local market—especially institutional customers—will continue to grow, and that these companies will aggressively pursue opportunities in other markets.

Looking to the future, some of the long-distance companies have announced plans to build their own local telephone networks in major cities in order to compete with the existing local telephone companies. Long-distance companies, including the smaller firms, may also lease capacity from the local carriers to resell services. An open question is whether this competition will concentrate on the largest and most lucrative customers—such as corporations in urban areas—or also extend to the residential market for basic telephone service.

Conversely, although long-distance companies already participate in a fairly competitive market, they are threatened by the possible entry of the RBOCs into the long-distance market. The RBOCs have the money, and the access to the customer, that could allow them to take a substantial share of the long-distance market quickly. The long-distance companies will work hard through the FCC, state public utility commissions, and perhaps also the courts to make sure that the RBOCs are not permitted to provide long-distance service until they face competition for local telephone service.

The long-distance companies are also diversifying into other lines of business. AT&T has purchased McCaw Cellular, the largest of all U.S. cellular communications companies, while Sprint has joined with a number of cable companies to purchase several of the new PCS wireless licenses. AT&T and MCI have both invested in direct broadcast satellite (DBS) services that provide video programming to the home in competition with cable companies. And both MCI and Sprint have received infusions of cash from foreign sources—MCI from British Telecom, while Sprint has developed financial links with Deutsche Telekom and France Telecom.

In short, like their local counterparts, the long-distance telephone companies are attempting to enter new markets to varying degrees, while simultaneously attempting to defend their existing turf from new market entrants. The telecommunications equipment manufacturers may have the most to gain from competition for local telephone and cable television services. In short, the more companies build competing networks, the more equipment they will buy.

While heavyweights such as IBM and Motorola still dominate the equipment industry, the market also consists of thousands of intermediate and smaller companies developing niche products. In contrast to the prevailing trends toward concentration, AT&T divested its equipment manufacturing arm into a new company called Lucent Technologies.

The equipment market is also the most international. Northern Telecom (Canada), Siemens (Germany), and Ericsson (Sweden) are actively involved in the U.S. market. The manufacturers face risks as well. The RBOCs are seeking permission under the Telecommunications Act of 1996 to engage in manufacturing. Some incumbent manufacturers are concerned that the RBOCs largely or exclusively will purchase equipment from their own subsidiaries, rather than purchasing it from independent suppliers as they do today.

Others, however, believe that the RBOCs will provide investment capital to a variety of manufacturers that will help them to develop new products—in short, that the market pie will not remain fixed in size and get divided up among more players, but rather that it will expand to provide opportunities for all players.

Manufacturers also have to be careful not to put all their eggs in one basket, as the market can shift quickly. The challenge for equipment makers is to anticipate the market so they are not, for instance, still selling fiber optic electronics if the world has shifted to wireless.

## Computer-based Service Providers

Computer-based information-service providers are increasingly important players in the contemporary environment. In essence, there are three major types of companies involved here: Internet access providers, which provide the general public with links to the global Internet; commercial on-line services like America Online, MSN, and Prodigy, which offer the general public both simple Internet access and also their own proprietary networks and content; and sophisticated business services like Electronic Data Systems, Dow Jones, and Dun and Bradstreet, which provide highly specialized and expensive proprietary systems and information to corporate and institutional clients.

The information-services business is one of the fastest growing parts of the communications marketplace. For example, over the past few years, Internet usage has been growing at rates of up to 20 percent per month. Informative, entertaining information content is of course one of the main attractions of the new media systems, be it the Internet, CD-ROMs, or proposed interactive television services.

Despite their centrality to the new communications environment in recent years, these companies are just beginning to pose a threat to the established players. For example, information-service companies are developing software that allows consumers to complete telephone calls over the Internet, at prices well below those of the telephone companies. Some companies are also experimenting with providing video services over computer networks, a step that would allow them to compete with cable television and direct broadcast satellite services.

Similarly, many advertisers are putting advertising on these computer information networks, which means that advertisers have less money to spend on broadcast and newspaper ads. In part because of this competition for revenues, the traditional newspaper and magazine industries are trying to develop their own computer information services.

The information-services companies face challenges as well as opportunities. Perhaps the biggest challenge is transmission speed. Especially with proprietary networks like America Online, the more popular the services become, the more usage of computer networks increases, and the slower the networks get for everyone. For the information services, obtaining reliable access to sufficient network capacity is emerging as a key concern.

Accordingly, information-services companies are now forming strategic partnerships with local telephone companies, long-distance telephone companies, cable television companies -- whoever can provide them the fastest transmission rates and most reliable connections. Such partnerships will become increasingly important to the information services in the future if they wish to hold onto their customers.

This is especially so if the information-service providers hope to prevent the telephone companies from taking over their business with separate service offerings. Cable television companies grew quickly in the 1980s, taking advantage of their status as unregulated monopolies. Unfortunately for them, their rate increases and poor service offended consumers so much that the U.S. Congress put them back under regulation and took away their monopoly in 1992.

As a result, cable companies are now beginning to face some competition from direct broadcast satellites and "wireless cable" services, which use microwave transmissions to deliver video programs to a home antenna. The cable industry is dominated by two main companies, TCI and Time-Warner. TCI, based in Denver, Colorado, provides cable service to approximately 23 percent of the cable market and has an investment interest in most of the popular cable television program stations that it carries over its cable networks.

Time-Warner has also taken over Turner Broadcasting, Inc., a move that will give it about as many cable subscribers as TCI. In addition, Time-Warner has acquired television stations, newspapers, and the film libraries of MGM studios, one of the major Hollywood movie studios. With their rates controlled by regulation and their growth stabilizing, cable television companies are eager to find new sources of revenue. First on their list is the local-telephone business.

Cable companies are exploring ways to carry telephone calls over the same wires they use to transmit television programs. But cable networks generally are built to transmit one-way television programs, and the costs of upgrading their networks to carry two-way telephone calls are high. Cable television companies may have more luck providing data transmission, such as access to the Internet, over their wires.

Rather than upgrade their new networks, several cable companies are purchasing local-telephone competitors. Several cable firms, including TCI, jointly purchased Teleport, an emerging competitor to the telephone companies in urban markets. Other cable companies have invested heavily in licenses for the new personal communications services.

Cable companies are facing small but growing competition from direct broadcast satellite (DBS) companies. DBS competitors acquired over 3.3 million customers in the past three years alone, primarily in rural areas. Rather than fight against DBS, the major cable operators are now trying to join them. Five of the biggest cable operators joined to form a consortium called Primestar to deliver satellite programming directly to the home.

Cable television companies also must prepare for competition from the local telephone companies in the video market. The telephone companies are having the same kind of problems upgrading their networks to provide cable service that the cable companies are having in providing telephone service. For this reason, several telephone companies recently decided to invest in wireless-cable services.

Since these wireless-cable companies do not need to lay wires directly to consumers' homes, they may be able to build competitive systems relatively quickly, at least in urban areas. The American broadcast industry consists of about 1,100 television stations and several thousand local radio stations. As a whole, the industry earns about 30 thousand million dollars per year, mostly in advertising.

Financial support from advertisers allows broadcasters to deliver their programs to the public for free. For years, industry analysts have been predicting the demise of broadcasting. Television and radio broadcasters essentially deliver the same type of product that they delivered 30 years ago.

Yet broadcasters provide the only source of local news, weather, and sports information in a format that is easily understood and attractive. As a result, broadcasters' revenues continue to grow despite the growth of new and competing technologies. Broadcasters face a number of threats, however. Local radio stations will face strong competition from a proposed satellite radio service capable of delivering digital signals to the entire country.

Television broadcasters are facing increasing competition from cable systems and wireless-cable systems, both of which can provide video programs to consumers' homes with higher-quality digital signals. In response, broadcasters are trying to make more efficient and flexible use of the radio frequency spectrum they use to provide new services. Broadcasters are developing high definition television (HDTV) systems that could allow them to transmit signals with twice the image clarity of conventional systems, as well as information services like sports scores and stock market data.

Indeed, in some visions of the future, the broadcasters could even use digital services conveyed through the spectrum to provide telephone calls in competition with the telephone, cable, and information-service companies. The transition to HDTV is tricky, however. HDTV is not compatible with existing broadcast technology. Consumers must be willing to spend the money to replace their existing television set with a new television set capable of receiving digital signals.

Until all viewers have purchased the new sets, broadcasters will continue to broadcast using the older format alongside the new HDTV format. Because of the uncertainties surrounding HDTV, some broadcasters are seeking to reduce their costs by enlarging and consolidating the number of stations they own.

The Telecommunications Act relaxed many of the limits on the number of radio and television stations any one entity may own, a change that has spawned a frenzy of purchases of broadcast stations. In addition, in 1995, two of the four major television networks (CBS and ABC) were sold for many thousands of millions of dollars. In short, broadcasters face increasing competition for their advertising revenues, but they deliver a product—local information and entertainment—that, so far, cannot be matched.

The electric utility companies are one of the oldest, and newest, players in telecommunications markets. Many of the electric utilities have deployed extensive fiber optic networks as part of the monitoring and control of their electrical systems. The utilities are trying to take advantage of the excess capacity on these fiber lines to generate additional revenues.

Electric companies first provided wholesale, bulk capacity to telecommunications carriers. Now they are applying to provide local telephone service themselves. While the electric companies do not have years of experience in telecommunications, they do have tremendous capital. Consumers spend as much if not more on energy services than they spend on telecommunications.

Even the telephone companies, usually the advocates of less regulation, have asked the FCC for regulatory protections against unfair competition from the electric companies. In sum, the U.S. market for telecommunications goods and services is growing at somewhere between 10 and 15 percent per year. The major companies cannot be satisfied with holding on to what they have; competition is certain to eat away at their market shares.

Many companies believe the key to their survival is to be able to provide several different communications services in one convenient package. Consumers like the convenience of obtaining all their communications services from one vendor—what some call "one-stop shopping." Companies are frantically entering alliances to line up their package of services now before they lose the opportunity. That is why the telephone companies are considering entering the video business, why long-distance telephone companies are investing in DBS and the Internet, and why computer services and newspapers are joining forces.

At the same time, the new competitive environment is creating opportunities for smaller entrepreneurs to develop niche products that fulfill needs that larger companies do not recognize. The companies that will prosper in the next century will be those that learn how to integrate these new technologies into a package of services that is the most convenient for the consumer.

## Assessment of Wireless Communication

Business needs access to high bandwidth facilities capable of dealing with the ever increasing volumes of data generated by Internet-related applications, and other bandwidth-hungry applications like video conferencing. Consumers will increasingly demand faster access to the myriad information, education and entertainment services offered by the Internet and also to new services like video on demand.

However, the cost of obtaining high bandwidth services via cable or fixed link radio technology is currently preventing widespread use of such services. An aim of releasing large allocations of spectrum is to enable the rapid deployment of high data rate services at lower prices than currently available. This should especially be the case in areas of low subscriber density, where the costs of laying cable would be prohibitive.

In UK, the Government believes that competition is the best way to deliver this access. Competition drives innovation. Competition reduces prices and increases choice. The Government wants to see competition both between different companies using the same broadband technologies and between different technologies.

The Government has already made several tranches of spectrum available for radio fixed access services:-

— At 10GHz, two licensed operators currently have access to 2 by 30MHz of spectrum. The intention was for these operators to use point-to-multipoint technology to provide higher data rate services principally to business customers;

— The Radiocommunications Agency will soon issue a consultation document on the licensing options for the use of spectrum previously assigned to Ionica at 3.4GHz and 10GHz. Licences are likely to be awarded in the near future for the provision of Fixed Wireless Access (FWA) services providing telephony, data and Internet services;

— Tele2 have been offered a licence to provide FWA services in the 4GHz band, subject to demonstrating that their systems can share with existing services in the band. Tele2 provide a range of data rates to their subscribers, including Internet access at rates above those currently obtainable with wireline techniques; and

— Atlantic Telecommunications are offering FWA services at 2.4GHz in parts of the country.

## Broadband Wireless Access

A more complete analysis of higher bandwidth demand issues is covered in the OFTEL document Access to Bandwidth along with an overview of the range of alternative wired and wireless platforms for delivering broadband interactive services. The business community have a major, and immediate, demand for access to spectrum in order to deliver and send information at bit-rates of 2Mbit/s and above between fixed points.

The whole range of interests, including telecommunications companies, current and potential operators and manufacturers were all enthusiastic about the existing and potential business market. Initial applications include high speed access to the Internet, remote local area network access, file and data transfer between companies and video-conferencing.

In the longer term, these demands are expected to extend to desk to desk video, tele-medicine, interactive computer aided design, greater collaborative working over the wireless networks and, of course, the development of electronic commerce enabling business to business and business to customer transactions.

The fact that many large organisations already have broadband connections through fibre, cable or fixed wireless point-to-point links. There appears to be a demand, however, for point-to-multipoint wireless links within private networks as well as a growing market among small and medium sized firms for a shared point to multipoint wireless system within public networks. Households will require access to broadband infrastructures for purposes such as video telephony, video-on-demand, broadcasting, home shopping and banking, tele-education, games, and high speed Internet access.

The availability of lower cost point to multipoint equipment will give a boost to these markets and mean that higher dater rates are available to a much larger number of businesses and consumers to use in new and innovative ways. The Government invites comments on the demand for broadband services and the level of interest in delivering services to customers over broadband fixed wireless networks in the context of the various other platforms.

In UK, the government wants to see a competitive and dynamic UK communications industry throughout the full service chain, covering network infrastructure, equipment, service provision and content. The Government looks to broadband developments to provide major manufacturing and export opportunities, keeping the UK at the leading edge of advanced communications developments.

Promoting competition in networks through the provision of radio spectrum for wireless networks will help to meet these ends providing new means of providing high bandwidth links to customers stimulating competition in both infrastructure and services. This Consultation Document considers two spectrum bands for the purpose of delivering Broadband Wireless Fixed Access by terrestrial means, 40.5 - 43.5GHz and 27.5 - 29.5GHz.

In terms of the Government's broad social and economic objectives, this bandwidth provides a major opportunity for the development of a wide range of genuinely innovative and advanced digital services, including in a domestic context. Moreover, the successful development of this band will provide a basis for exploiting even higher reaches of the radio spectrum. There is sufficient bandwidth in the 40GHz band to provide capacity for domestic applications such as video entertainment services which require high bandwidth to be available for long periods, as well as for transactional or internet style traffic involving shorter bursts of data, which may be the primary need of small and medium sized businesses (SMEs).

The bandwidth advantages at 40GHz may offset any suggested difficulties arising from the need to use smaller cells compared with other bands. Bandwidth constraints will probably soon become a problem at lower bands, even for SMEs, while assuming such an architecture, the optimum cell sizes will be limited more by capacity constraints than propagation characteristics. Manufacturers have been developing 40GHz technology over a number of years.

Some study shows that demand tends to expand to fill or exceed the available bandwidth. Even domestic consumers will increasingly require larger upstream channels. This implies that all broadband networks need to be planned flexibly with the capability of varying degrees of asymmetry in the capacity of forward and back channels. Currently, the frequency band 40.5GHz to 42.5GHz is allocated globally in the Radio Regulations of the International Telecommunication Union (ITU) to the Fixed Service (including broadband wireless fixed access) along with the (terrestrial) Broadcasting Service and Broadcasting-Satellite Service on a co-primary basis, i.e. with equal rights.

In many parts of the world, outside Europe, the band is also allocated provisionally to the Fixed Satellite

Service (space to Earth links). This provisional allocation is due to come into force from 1st January 2001 and is currently being reviewed in the ITU in the context of the requirements of other services in this, and neighbouring, bands and the results of sharing studies.

The next World Radio Conference (WRC) in 2000 will consider this issue and also, possibly, a global Fixed-Satellite allocation, including the UK, in the band. This could potentially complicate the use of this band for broadband wireless fixed access. The frequency band 42.5GHz to 43.5GHz is allocated in the Radio Regulations to the Fixed Service along with the Fixed-Satellite Service (Earth to space), the Mobile Service and Radioastronomy on a co-primary basis. There is a specific need in this band for administrations to take steps to protect the radioastronomy service from harmful interference, which will affect the availability of spectrum in some parts of the country for broadband wireless fixed access.

### Broadcasting Spectrum Issues

Certainly, the bandwidth at 40GHz has the capacity to sustain such services and some potential operators have mooted the possibility of a mixture of broadcasting and broadband telecommunications services. The Government is minded not to exclude the provision of broadcasting services over broadband wireless networks. In certain areas of the country local delivery operators (LDOs) have access to the 40.5 to 42.5GHz band for wireless cable broadcasting. Licensees in this category cover some 25% of the population.

The development of broadband technology in general, and digital in particular, together with the development of the cable companies as telecommunications operators, has altered significantly the circumstances in which this spectrum was originally made available to the Independent Television Commission (ITC) under the terms of the Broadcasting Act 1990.

The spectrum was provided to enable the provision of analogue broadcasting services in less urbanised areas and to enable early roll out of networks prior to cable installation. Spectrum was allocated in a pre-digital, early satellite era when alternative broadcasting choice was more limited, while the cable companies were primarily broadcasters and not telecommunications operators.

The development of competition in the broadcasting and telecommunications markets, which the Government wishes to promote further, together with the need to ensure most efficient use and management of the radio spectrum has led the Government to reconsider the allocation of this spectrum to the ITC.

From the Government's perspective, in areas where companies have already laid cable or where the companies' licences under the Broadcasting Act preclude the use of radio, there is no reason why the spectrum should not be redeployed for broadband wireless access. Where those LDOs have no intention to use the radio spectrum in their franchise areas it would be beneficial to redeploy this spectrum for other uses such as Interactive Multimedia Services.

Not all of these Broadcasting Act licensees will wish to exercise the option of seeking licences under the Wireless Telegraphy Act to use MVDS technology to supplement or replace roll-out of their wire based cable networks, or would only wish to do so in part of their franchise areas. The Government will invite the ITC to clarify the intentions of the LDOs to use wireless in their franchise areas. Spectrum pricing under the Wireless Telegraphy Act 1998 could also be applied to give an incentive to LDOs to use or relinquish spectrum. This will be the subject of a separate consultation document concerning spectrum pricing across the Broadcasting Sector.

Some operators have suggested that an early initiative at 28GHz will be focused on the immediate needs of specific business markets, say using duplex channels of 56MHz. This would preclude large scale provision of bandwidth-hungry domestic entertainment services such as video-on-demand.

SME customers may be satisfied with capacity of 2Mbits per second at present although the demand would be likely to grow in time. Allocations of spectrum at 28GHz could not support the network capacity and density envisaged for full service access networks but could prepare the market for such larger scale requirements.

With the potential introduction of large scale non-geostationary fixed satellite systems and geostationary satellite systems in parts of the band, there has been considerable activity to study the issue of sharing between the co-primary services. This work continues within the European regulatory bodies and the ITU.

The Government believes that standardisation plays an important role in the development of communications services. In general the standardisation process is best dealt with through voluntary co-operation by industry groups with standards which emerge then adopted formally, where appropriate, in formal standards making bodies.

Licences for major independent broadcasting services have been made available through either a form of auction process or through a comparative selection process. Licences for wireless public networks at 10GHz were made available prior to the Wireless Telegraphy Act 1998 through a beauty competition while it is planned that licences for third generation mobile telecommunications will be made available by auction using powers introduced by the 1998 Act.

In general, a properly designed spectrum auction with a significant number of well prepared bidders should ensure that spectrum is made available to those who value it most, and who will use it most valuably, thus producing the greatest economic benefit. This can be achieved by an appropriate auction design that puts information on bids into the public domain and allows other bidders to react. The alternative, involving a comparative selection process, tends to favour incumbents and is less transparent and objective.

In view of the market and technology uncertainty, Quotient, among others, have noted the advantages of issuing early licences using a portion of the spectrum on a "Pioneer" basis before allocating the full amount of spectrum. Such an approach would achieve an early path to licences and help to "inform" the market about the commercial possibilities of broadband wireless and the robustness and maturity of the technology. The pioneers would also serve to accelerate the technology into wider commercial use. These "early starters" would be charged, initially at least, a "limited" fee reflecting the uncertain and high costs of setting up networks and the inevitable technology introduction problems.

However, the pioneer approach presents considerable difficulties - including the choice of licence packages, how to select licensees in an objective, transparent and non-discriminatory way, and how to price the spectrum. Pioneer licences can also be regarded as anticompetitive as they give holders an inside track to the spectrum and to markets.

The number of licences made available will be determined by decisions on the bandwidth to provide to each operator. Of course, the spectrum in both bands can be permutated and combined on an area basis as well as by bandwidth. In general, it is desirable to ensure there is a sufficient number of operators to provide genuine competition.

A substantial majority of responses to the Radiocommunications Agency's consultative document Managing Spectrum through the Market favoured spectrum trading. However, such a development would require legislation which could take several years. The European Commission is currently consulting on whether to amend the EU Licensing Directive to facilitate spectrum trading and the Radiocommunications Agency will be developing proposals, in consultation with industry, for the necessary changes to UK law.

The value of licences increases with their duration and security of tenure. The considerations affecting the choice of licence duration include the time required for marketing, rollout, the time taken for networks to mature and markets to stabilise, and the time over which networks might become obsolete as new technologies advance.

# Bibliography

Banket, V. L., and V. M. Dorofeev, *Digital Methods in Satellite Communications*, Moscow: Radio & Svyaz, 1988.

Bar, Francois, et al. 1999, "Defending the Internet Revolution in the Broadband Era: When Doing Nothing Is Doing Harm," August, 1999.

Beniger, James, *The Control Revolution: Technological and Economic Origins of the Information Society*, Harvard University Press, Cambridge, Mass.: 1986.

Beierle, Thomas, and Sarah Cahill Electronic Democracy and Environmental Governance: A Survey of the States, Resources for the Future, *Discussion Paper 00-42*, October 2000, 30 p.

Bennahum, David S, "The Myth of Digital Nirvana." *Educomm Review 31.5* (September/October 1996).

Berkowe, Kathleen Hawkins, 2000, "Open Access to Cable Systems for Internet Access Providers", Media Law and Policy VIII (2).

Berman, Dennis, and Shawn Young, 2001, "Bells Make a High-Speed Retreat from Broadband", Wall Street Journal. October 29, p. B1.

Bland, Sir Christopher, President of the BBC, "Meeting the Challenges", *EBU Diffusion*, Autumn 1996, p. 6.

Bonime, A., and K. C., Pohlmann, *Writing for New Media: The essential guide to writing for interactive media, CD-ROMs, and the Web*, New York: John Wiley and Sons, 1998.

Bourgault, L. M., *Mass Media in Sub-Saharan Africa*, Bloomington, Ind., 1995, p. 127.

Carrolll, R, L., et al., "Consonance in Local Television News Program Content: An Examination of Intermarket Diversity", *Journal of Broadcasting and Electronic Media*, Vol. 41, No. 1, Winter, 1997, pp. 132–44.

CCIR: *Handbook on satellite communications* (fixed satellite service), International Telecommunications Union, Geneva, 1985.

Center for Democracy and Technology (CDT), 2000, Broadband Backgrounder: Public Policy Issues Raised by Broadband Technology, Washington, D.C.: CDT, December.

Center for Media Education (CME), 2001, "Broadband Networks and Narrow Visions: The Internet at Risk." Washington, D.C.: CME.

Centerwall, B.S., "Exposure to television as a cause of violence," in Comstock G., (ed) *Public Communications as Behavior*, Orlando, FL: Academic Press, Inc., 1989.

Mander, Jerry, *Four Arguments for the Elimination of Television*, New York: Morrow, 1977.

McLuhan, Marshall, *Understanding Media: The Extensions of Man*, New York: McGraw-Hill, 1964.

# Index